The Federal Government

THE LEGISLATIVE BRANCH

Creating America's Laws

Tony Zurlo

MyReportLinks.com Books

an imprint of

 Enslow Publishers, Inc.

Box 398, 40 Industrial Road
Berkeley Heights, NJ 07922
USA

MyReportLinks.com Books, an imprint of Enslow Publishers, Inc. MyReportLinks®
is a registered trademark of Enslow Publishers, Inc.

Library of Congress Cataloging-in-Publication Data

Zurlo, Tony.
  The legislative branch : creating America's laws / Tony Zurlo.
      p. cm. — (The federal government)
  Includes bibliographical references and index.
  ISBN-13: 978-1-59845-056-9
  ISBN-10: 1-59845-056-5
  1. United States. Congress—Juvenile literature. I. Title.
JK1025.Z87 2008
328.73—dc22

                                        2006023127

Printed in the United States of America

10 9 8 7 6 5 4 3 2 1

To Our Readers:
Through the purchase of this book, you and your library gain access to the Report Links that specifically back up this book.
The Publisher will provide access to the Report Links that back up this book and will keep these Report Links up to date on **www.myreportlinks.com** for five years from the book's first publication date.
We have done our best to make sure all Internet addresses in this book were active and appropriate when we went to press. However, the author and the Publisher have no control over, and assume no liability for, the material available on those Internet sites or on other Web sites they may link to.
The usage of the MyReportLinks.com Books Web site is subject to the terms and conditions stated on the Usage Policy Statement on **www.myreportlinks.com.**
A password may be required to access the Report Links that back up this book. The password is found on the bottom of page 4 of this book.
Any comments or suggestions can be sent by e-mail to comments@myreportlinks.com or to the address on the back cover.

Photo Credits: AP/Wide World Photos, pp. 66–67, 70–71; Architect of the Capitol, p. 21; Arizona State University College of Law, p. 111; Cable News Network, p. 15; Citizens Against Government Waste, p. 100; Clemson University, p. 49; Common Cause, p. 36; © Corel Corporation, pp. 1, 3, 106–107, 112; Dirksen Congressional Center, p. 22; Electronic Frontier Foundation, p. 104; *Harper's* Magazine Foundation, p. 102; LBJ Library Collection, pp. 98–99; Library of Congress, pp. 8–9, 10, 30, 42, 56–57, 60–61, 75, 78, 82, 88–89; Long Island University, p. 51; Margaret Chase Smith Library, p. 94; MyReportLinks.com Books, p. 4; National Archives, pp. 43, 65; National Park Service, p. 59; National Security Agency/Central Security Service, p. 12; New Deal Network, p. 63; Office of the Clerk, U.S. House of Representatives, pp. 73, 93; © 1999 PhotoDisc, pp. 18–19; Photos.com, p. 31; Richard Nixon Library & Birthplace, p. 24; Shutterstock.com, p. 7; The Henry Clay Memorial Foundation, 2001, p. 45; The Official Web site of Hillary Rodham Clinton, p. 96; The Official Web site of Robert C. Byrd, p. 85; The Texas State Historical Association, p. 80; 2003–07 Country Studies US, p. 86; University of Missouri-Kansas City Law School, p. 53; University of South Dakota, p. 84; U.S. Department of the Interior, pp. 46–47; U.S. General Services Administration's Office of Citizen Services and Communications, p. 114; U.S. Government Printing Office, p. 34; U.S. House of Representatives, p. 25; U.S. Senate, pp. 29, 38, 91.

Cover Photo: © Corel Corporation (Capitol building); United States Congress (seal).

Contents

MyReportLinks.com Books
Great Books, Great Links, Great for Research!

APPROVED WEB SITE

The Internet sites featured in this book can save you hours of research time. These Internet sites—we call them **"Report Links"**—are constantly changing, but we keep them up to date on our Web site.

When you see this "Approved Web Site" logo, you will know that we are directing you to a great Internet site that will help you with your research.

Give it a try! Type http://www.myreportlinks.com into your browser, click on the series title and enter the password, then click on the book title, and scroll down to the Report Links listed for this book.

The Report Links will bring you to great source documents, photographs, and illustrations. MyReportLinks.com Books save you time, feature Report Links that are kept up to date, and make report writing easier than ever! A complete listing of the Report Links can be found on pages 116–117 at the back of the book.

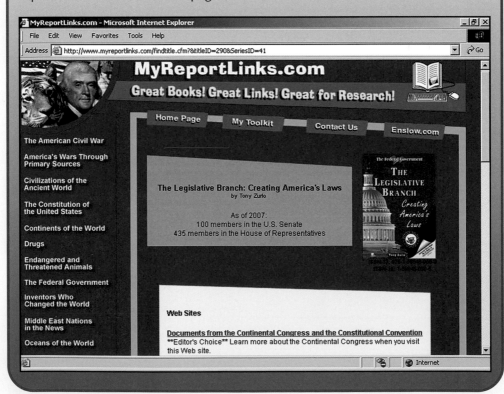

Please see "To Our Readers" on the copyright page for important information about this book, the MyReportLinks.com Web site, and the Report Links that back up this book.

Please enter **LBA1943** if asked for a password.

Time Line

1776 —The Second Continental Congress signs the Declaration of Independence.

1787 —Thirty-nine men from thirteen states sign the final draft of the Constitution.

1789 —The first modern Congress meets in New York City.

1803 —Congress approves President Thomas Jefferson's purchase of the Louisiana Territory.

1820 —Missouri Compromise passes. It attempts to balance political power between slave and free states.

1833 —Congress agrees to compromise on the tariff bill that keeps the South and North unified.

1850 —The Compromise of 1850 allows the slave and free states to remain unified.

1861 –1865 —The Civil War is fought in the United States between the North (Union) and the South (Confederacy).

1865 —Slavery is abolished by the Thirteenth Amendment passed by Congress.

1866 —Republicans take control of Reconstruction of the South. From 1866 to 1870 they pass a civil rights law and two Constitutional amendments (Fourteenth and Fifteenth) that promise equal rights to African Americans.

1868 —Republicans try, but fail to impeach President Andrew Johnson falling one vote shy of a two-thirds majority in the Senate.

1870 —Congress expands rapidly from the population growth in the United States. This results in many more congressional committees to deal with the increased legislation. This is also a period of increased power for the House Speaker.

1890 –1920 —Congress passes several bills that promote the health and safety of Americans. This era is often called the Progressive Era.

1916 —Jeannette Rankin of Montana becomes the first woman elected to the House of Representatives.

1918 —The Nineteenth Amendment, granting women the right to vote, is passed.

1920 —The Nineteenth Amendment becomes law.

1930s —The Great Depression leads to Democratic control of Congress. Congress cooperates with Democratic president Franklin D. Roosevelt to pass laws that help bring the nation out of the Depression.

1932 —Hattie Wyatt Caraway of Arkansas becomes the first woman elected to the Senate.

Time Line (cont.)

1933 —Democrats begin their near sixty-year control of Congress. Republicans will be the majority in the House only in 1946–47 and 1952–53, and in the Senate in 1953–55 and from 1981–85.

1940s —A Democratic Congress works closely with President Roosevelt to pass bills that support America's war efforts in World War II.

1940 –1961 —Representative Sam Rayburn of Texas is Speaker during much of this period. He works closely with both parties to gain legislation.

1950s —Senator Lyndon B. Johnson of Texas is the majority leader for most of this decade. He is able to get both parties to compromise on legislation.

1964 —Congress passes the Civil Rights Act. This act guarantees equal access for all people to public facilities such as parks, hotels, and restaurants. The act also promises equal job opportunities to all races.

—Congress passes the Gulf of Tonkin Resolution giving President Johnson permission to attack targets in North Vietnam. This begins the buildup of American troops in the Vietnam War.

1967 —Massachusetts Senator Edward Brooke III is the first African American elected to the Senate since the Reconstruction era.

1974 —Congress investigates crimes committed by the advisors of President Richard Nixon. When Congress is about to impeach the president, Nixon resigns from office.

1981 —Republicans are the majority in the Senate for the first time since 1955.

1994 —Newt Gingrich guides Republicans to victory in November elections. For the first time since 1954, they take control of both houses in 1995.

1995 —Except for the 107th Congress (2001–03) Republicans are the majority party through the 109th Congress (2005–06).

1999 —The Senate acquits President Bill Clinton of impeachment charges.

2001 —Congress passes the Patriot Act one month after the 9/11 attacks in New York City and Arlington, Virginia, to help the government find terrorists.

—September 18: Congress passes a resolution authorizing the United States Armed Forces to take action against anyone responsible for the 9/11 attacks.

2002 —October: Congress adopts a joint resolution called the Authorization for Use of Military Force Against Iraq Resolution of 2002.

2003 —March 10: United States forces invade Iraq.

2006 —After three years of war in Iraq, Congress begins to question whether President George W. Bush has a clear plan for the war against terrorists.

WAR ON TERROR

1

On September 11, 2001, al-Qaeda terrorists attacked New York's World Trade Center and the Pentagon in Arlington, Virginia. Americans, and most of the world, called for the destruction of al-Qaeda. Senator Richard Shelby of Alabama, the top Republican on the Senate Intelligence Committee, declared, "[W]e're gonna hunt you [al-Qaeda terrorists] down and we're gonna find you and we're gonna make you pay that price."[1]

⟶ CONGRESS APPROVES FORCE TO FIGHT TERRORISM

The Constitution gives Congress the duty of declaring war. As commander in chief

A man covered with ashes aids a woman who is having trouble breathing after the attacks on the World Trade Center on September 11, 2001. The 9/11 attacks initiated a flurry of legislation in Congress.

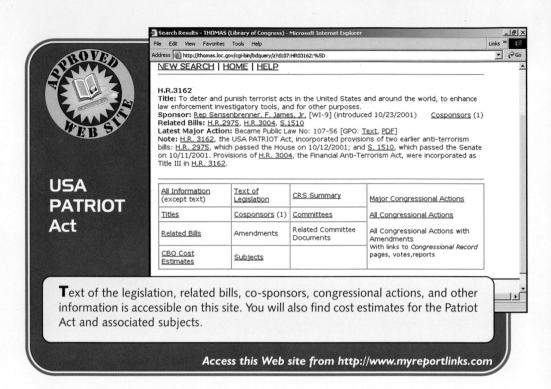

USA PATRIOT Act

File Edit View Favorites Tools Help

Links »

Address http://thomas.loc.gov/cgi-bin/bdquery/z?d107:HR03162:%5D Go

NEW SEARCH | HOME | HELP

H.R.3162
Title: To deter and punish terrorist acts in the United States and around the world, to enhance law enforcement investigatory tools, and for other purposes.
Sponsor: Rep Sensenbrenner, F. James, Jr. [WI-9] (introduced 10/23/2001)   Cosponsors (1)
Related Bills: H.R.2975, H.R.3004, S.1510
Latest Major Action: Became Public Law No: 107-56 [GPO: Text, PDF]
Note: H.R. 3162, the USA PATRIOT Act, incorporated provisions of two earlier anti-terrorism bills: H.R. 2975, which passed the House on 10/12/2001; and S. 1510, which passed the Senate on 10/11/2001. Provisions of H.R. 3004, the Financial Anti-Terrorism Act, were incorporated as Title III in H.R. 3162.

All Information (except text)	Text of Legislation	CRS Summary	Major Congressional Actions
Titles	Cosponsors (1)	Committees	All Congressional Actions
Related Bills	Amendments	Related Committee Documents	All Congressional Actions with Amendments
CBO Cost Estimates	Subjects		With links to *Congressional Record* pages, votes,reports

Text of the legislation, related bills, co-sponsors, congressional actions, and other information is accessible on this site. You will also find cost estimates for the Patriot Act and associated subjects.

Access this Web site from http://www.myreportlinks.com

of the military, the president's job is to manage how a war is fought. As a rule, presidents ask Congress to vote to go to war. In the past, the United States fought wars against countries that attacked America or our allies. After 9/11, Americans faced an enemy with loyalty to no country. This was, as Senator John Kerry of Massachusetts said, "a completely new, different kind of war from any we've fought previously."[2]

The Taliban government in Afghanistan sheltered al-Qaeda. So, Congress backed President Bush's plan to go after the Taliban. Many nations joined the United States to defeat the Taliban in December 2001. But al-Qaeda survived. Its leaders hid in the mountains that border Afghanistan and Pakistan.

For the next year, the Bush government said Iraq was tied to the 9/11 attackers. The administration also said that Iraq had weapons of mass destruction (WMD). They feared that Iraq might offer WMD to al-Qaeda for future strikes against Americans. Most of Congress believed the president and his advisors. So Congress passed the Authorization for Use of Military Force Against Iraq (AUMF) Resolution in October 2002. The bill permits the president to use military force against Iraq. So on March 10, 2003, United States forces invaded Iraq.

⊜Congress Passes the Patriot Act

Congress passed the Foreign Intelligence Surveillance Act (FISA) in October 1978. The intent of the act was to limit the president's power to spy on Americans in this country. The FISA requires the president to get a warrant from a special court called the United States Foreign Intelligence Surveillance Court (FISC) within seventy-two hours of starting a surveillance.

The 9/11 terrorists lived in the United States when they attacked. Americans questioned why officials had not discovered the terrorists before they struck. So in October 2001, Congress passed the Patriot Act to help the government find terrorists.

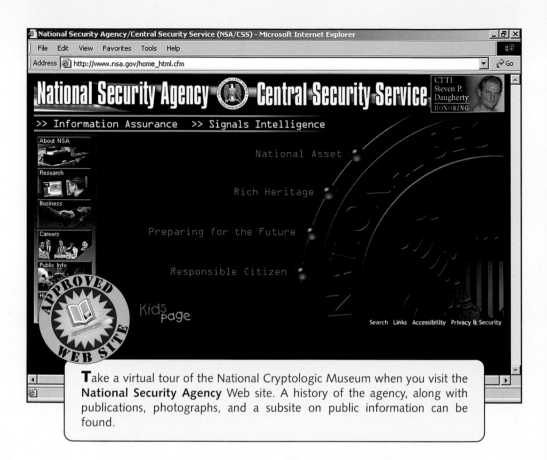

National Security Agency/Central Security Service (NSA/CSS) - Microsoft Internet Explorer

File   Edit   View   Favorites   Tools   Help

Address   http://www.nsa.gov/home_html.cfm   Go

National Security Agency   Central Security Service   CTT1 Steven P. Daugherty HONORING

>> Information Assurance   >> Signals Intelligence

About NSA

Research

Business

Careers

Public Info

Hi

APPROVED WEB SITE

National Asset

Rich Heritage

Preparing for the Future

Responsible Citizen

Kids page

Search Links Accessibility Privacy & Security

Take a virtual tour of the National Cryptologic Museum when you visit the **National Security Agency** Web site. A history of the agency, along with publications, photographs, and a subsite on public information can be found.

The Patriot Act amended parts of FISA. The FBI's budget to fight terrorists was increased. The act also made it easier for the FBI to record suspects' messages. It also gave more freedom to law enforcement across the United States. They could now share personal information about terror suspects. The act also helped the government track down those who financed terrorism.

→TERRORIST SURVEILLANCE PROGRAM

The Patriot Act was only part of the government's plan to find terrorists. The president set up a secret plan in early 2002 to find "terrorists plotting within our borders."[3] He wanted the ability to act quickly without telling Congress or the courts.

The Terrorist Surveillance Program (TSP) gave more power to the National Security Agency (NSA). Until then, the NSA could only spy on potential enemies overseas. The program allowed the NSA to monitor and record international phone calls and e-mails of people living in the United States with suspected ties to al-Qaeda. The program was kept secret so that terrorists would not know about it.

➔CONGRESS CHALLENGES THE TSP

In December 2005, *The New York Times* exposed the TSP in a front-page story.[4] Both Democrats and Republicans were upset. They argued that the President should have conferred with Congress first. They demanded that President Bush justify the program. He claimed that it applied only to people in the United States who make or receive calls from suspected members of al-Qaeda.[5]

Many members of Congress were skeptical. They claimed the president had no right to spy on Americans in the United States without permission from a judge. Members of Congress said they had a duty to monitor any program that deals with Americans' freedoms.

Many Americans believe that the TSP violates the Fourth Amendment, which says Americans are safe from "unreasonable searches and seizures" by the government. Officials must obtain written permission from a judge that describes the suspicious activity, "the place to be searched, and the persons or things to be seized."[6]

⊖DUBAI PORTS WORLD CONTROVERSY

Until the end of 2005, Congress backed President Bush in the fight against terrorism. But in early 2006, Congress began to question the President's plans. The press wrote about a government plan to allow a business owned by the United Arab Emirates (UAE) to manage parts of some American ports. The business was called Dubai Ports World (DP World).

At first, the press listed the ports of New York, New Jersey, Philadelphia, Baltimore, Miami, and New Orleans. Soon the press learned that DP World's job would be more extensive. DP World would also gain control over the loading and unloading of ships in nearly two dozen other ports in the United States from Maine to Texas.

Members of Congress heard from thousands of concerned voters. They wondered if a UAE-owned company would expose American ports to terrorists. Two of the 9/11 hijackers were from the UAE. And more than half of the money used by nineteen

9/11 hijackers ($125,000) had come from banks in Dubai. The press revealed that Iran, Libya, and North Korea got much of their nuclear technology through a Dubai firm. These concerns led Congress to propose legislation that would forbid the deal. As a result, DP World decided to sell all of its interests in United States ports.

⊖CHECKS AND BALANCES

The TSP and DP World conflicts raised the issue of checks and balances. The Founding Fathers sought to prevent any one person or group from having

Security concerns were raised over the prospect of having a foreign firm take over the management of American seaports. Read more about it in this online article called **"Bush Faces Pressure to Block Port Deal."**

unlimited power. So they gave each branch of government power to check the other branches.

Presidents tend to have more power in time of war. People want Congress to back the president in fights against an enemy. But in times of peace, Congress often demands a strong voice in making national policies.

In the spring of 2006, Congress tried to reclaim its influence over foreign policy. Bush and his supporters continued to resist. They believe presidents should have more power to act without consulting Congress, even when there is no declared war.[7] Members of Congress insist that the Constitution gives them an equal voice in decisions about national issues.

CONGRESS: ORGANIZATION AND RESPONSIBILITIES

2

Congress, or the legislative branch, is one of the three governing branches of the United States. The other two are the executive, led by the president; and the judicial, a national system of courts with the Supreme Court at the top.

Congress is made up of two houses. The "lower" house is the House of Representatives. The "upper" house is the Senate. By current law there are 435 members of the House of Representatives. Each state is divided into districts according to population. The bigger the state, the more representatives it has in the House. Representatives serve for two years. Then they must be reelected if they want to continue to serve.

The Senate is different. The United States Constitution gives each state two senators. They serve six-year terms. Every two years, the terms of one

The Capitol building, with its famous rotunda, is one of the most majestic looking government buildings in the entire world.

third of the one hundred senators are finished. If they wish to continue to serve, they must run for reelection.

Every year in early January, Congress meets in separate chambers in the Capitol building. They remain until late August or September. During this time they discuss, propose, and vote on laws that govern the lives of Americans. These assemblies of Congress are called sessions. Each session covers two years.

BALANCE OF POWER

The writers of the Constitution wanted to prevent any single person or group from having too much power. James Madison wrote that "The accumulation of all powers, legislative, executive, and judiciary, in the same hands, whether of one, a few, or many, . . . may justly be pronounced the very definition of tyranny."[1] To reach their goal, the Founding Fathers created a system of government that allocated powers among the three branches.

The legislative branch has the primary duty of passing laws that govern the nation. But the Founding Fathers wanted Congress to act cautiously. They encouraged debate and compromise before voting on a bill. They also required both houses to approve of each bill.

Even after Congress passes a bill, it does not become law. There are several ways for the other two branches to monitor, reject, or invalidate acts of Congress. This system is called "checks and balances."

The president can veto the bill once it is passed by Congress. After a veto, the bill returns to Congress. At least two thirds of each house must override the president's veto for it to become law. The courts are a second check on Congress's powers. Americans can challenge laws passed by Congress in the courts. Judges then decide if a law follows constitutional rules. Sometimes these challenges are taken to the highest court, the U. S. Supreme Court. There the justices make final decisions on whether or not laws follow constitutional guidelines.

➔HOUSE AND SENATE CHAMBERS

Congress meets in the Capitol building in Washington, D.C. It is five floors high, 751 feet (229 meters) long, and 350 feet (107 meters) wide. From ground level to the top of the Statue of Freedom atop the Dome is 288 feet (88 meters). The north wing of the building serves as the Senate

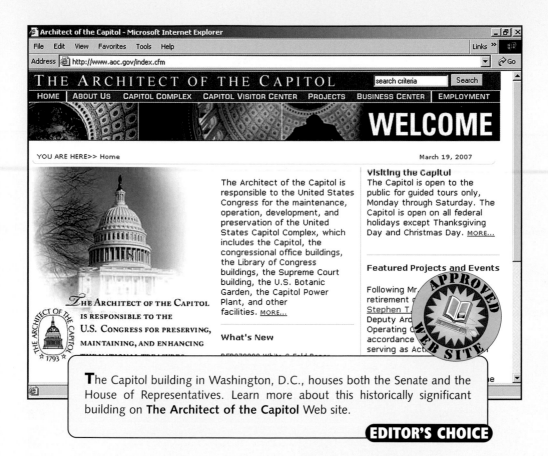

The Capitol building in Washington, D.C., houses both the Senate and the House of Representatives. Learn more about this historically significant building on **The Architect of the Capitol** Web site.

EDITOR'S CHOICE

chamber. The south wing is the House chamber. Circled around the edges of the chambers above the floor are galleries where the public and the press can sit during sessions.

The House chamber has long rows of seats divided by aisles. The seats all face the speaker's rostrum. Members can sit anywhere. But by tradition, Democrats sit to the right of the rostrum and Republicans to the left. Often the members gather in small groups to discuss bills. The room is noisy and seems disorganized to those not use to it.

Most of the time there are only a few of the 435 members present. They are often meeting in small committees to debate bills. They also leave the floor to greet visitors from their home districts. When a vote is scheduled, a buzzer rings in committee rooms, offices, and in the Capitol. This is to remind members to return to the floor to vote.

The Senate chamber is different. There are only one hundred members, so the atmosphere is usually calmer and "more relaxed" than the House.[2] The desks rise from the podium at one end of the chamber in four rows. Senators are assigned desks according to their length of service. Newest senators are seated in the back. The

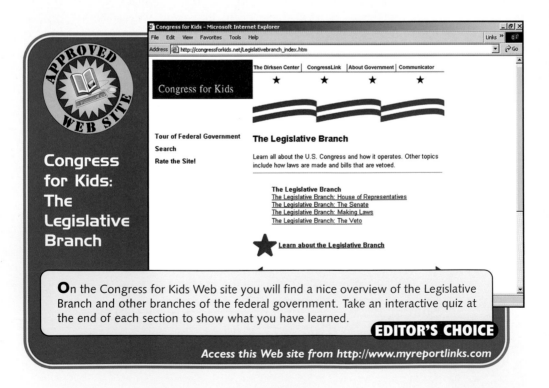

Congress for Kids: The Legislative Branch

On the Congress for Kids Web site you will find a nice overview of the Legislative Branch and other branches of the federal government. Take an interactive quiz at the end of each section to show what you have learned.

EDITOR'S CHOICE

Access this Web site from http://www.myreportlinks.com

longer the service, the closer a senator sits to the podium where the presiding officer sits.

Senators are often away tending to other business. Barack Obama, Democrat from Illinois, explains that "Except for the few minutes that it takes to vote, my colleagues and I don't spend much time on the Senate floor." Most senators are busy "juggling twelve or thirteen-hour schedules and want to get back to their offices to meet constituents or return phone calls, to a nearby hotel to cultivate donors, or to the television station for a live interview."[3] Like House members, senators are called back to votes on the Senate floor by buzzers located around the building and in their offices.

⊖Major Duties of Congress

The Constitution gives Congress clear duties called expressed powers. It also gives Congress the right to pass laws that are "necessary and proper" to carry out all the powers of the federal government.[4] This means that Congress has some ability to check the actions of the president and the courts. Almost all officials appointed by the president must be approved by Congress. This includes federal judges.

Congress can act as a court and jury to remove a judge considered unfit for office. The House must decide on the charges. This process is called impeachment. Then the Senate acts as the court to determine the judge's guilt or innocence.

Richard Nixon takes a stroll with his wife, Pat. Congress has the power to investigate the actions of the president. The Senate Watergate hearings, in which Nixon was questioned about his role in a break-in, is one example.

The House also has the power to charge the president or vice president with violating the law. The Chief Justice of the Supreme Court then presides over the hearing in the Senate. The House has impeached two presidents: Andrew Johnson and William Clinton. However, neither man was convicted by the Senate.

Congress's judicial power includes the investigation of the executive branch of government. The most famous case in recent times was the 1973 Senate Watergate hearings. President Richard

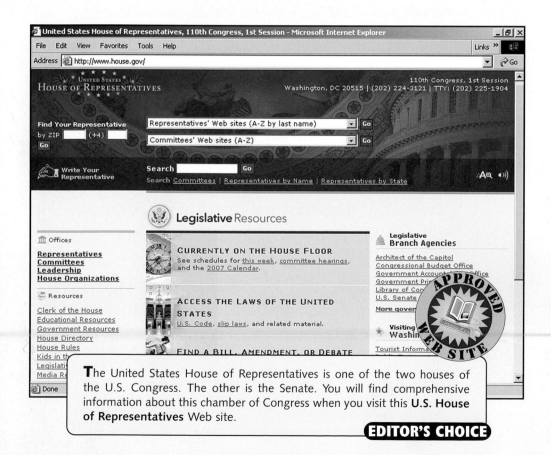

The United States House of Representatives is one of the two houses of the U.S. Congress. The other is the Senate. You will find comprehensive information about this chamber of Congress when you visit this **U.S. House of Representatives** Web site.

EDITOR'S CHOICE

Nixon resigned from office rather than face impeachment by Congress.

Other investigations by Congress involve issues that affect the public. In the early 1950s, the Kefauver hearings led to the arrest of many organized crime leaders. In such hearings, Congress can require witnesses to testify or be punished. Congress can also recommend that criminal charges be presented in the federal courts.

Congress also has the duty to supervise federal agencies and executive offices. This process is called oversight. Congressional committees are made up of members who study issues closely. The committees require agencies to report regularly on their programs.

→LEADERSHIP POSITIONS IN THE HOUSE OF REPRESENTATIVES

Each party elects its leaders for both the House and Senate. The leader of the party in power is called the majority leader, and the opposition party leader is called the minority leader. They are among the most influential politicians in Congress.

However, in the House the most powerful person is the Speaker. Before 1995, the Speakers of the House could serve as long as their party supported them. Since then, they have been limited to a total of eight years in the office. The Speaker in the 109th Congress was Republican Dennis

Hastert of Illinois. He was first elected Speaker by his party in 1999.

⊖SPEAKERS AND WHIPS

Speakers wield great power because of their party's majority. They appoint committee members and assign bills to committees for study. They also schedule bills for debate and vote on the House floor. This gives them the power to determine which bills the House membership will vote on. House Speakers are supported in their work by the House majority leader and the majority whip. Their job is to rally party members to unite to support bills and other party matters. In 2006, the Republican majority leader was Ohio congressman John Boehner and the majority whip was Missouri congressman Roy Blunt.

The minority party is the party with the second most members in each house of Congress. It is led in the House of Representatives by the minority leader and the minority whip. Their responsibilities are similar to that of the majority leader's. The minority leader in 2006 was Democrat Nancy Pelosi from California, the first woman elected as leader of her party in Congress. The minority whip in 2006 was Steny Hoyer of Maryland.

Things changed in 2007 because of the results of the November 2006 elections. In 2007, Nancy Pelosi became Speaker of the House and Steny Hoyer rose to House majority whip.

→LEADERSHIP POSITIONS IN THE SENATE

Vice presidents are the presidents of the Senate. However, the vice presidents rarely go to the Senate floor. Their most important duty is to vote when bills are tied. The president pro tempore presides over the daily business of the Senate. As a rule, this person is the most senior member of the majority party. Robert C. Byrd from West Virginia held this position in the 110th Congress. It is a position of high honor, but without much political strength.

The real power in the Senate is the majority leader. This person is elected by the party in control. In the 110th Congress, Harry Reid from Nevada held this position. With only one hundred members to deal with, the majority leader knows everyone on the floor from both major parties. As a result, the majority leader is able to work closely with them.

Majority leaders have lots of power. They speak for the party in control of the Senate. So their main duty is to convince senators to pass the party's program. They meet often with committee chairs to decide the workload for the Senate. When several senators want to speak, the majority leader has the right to speak first. This is called "right of first recognition." Majority leaders can offer amendments to bills. They can also change

U.S. Senate - Microsoft Internet Explorer

File   Edit   View   Favorites   Tools   Help   Links »

Address http://www.senate.gov/   Go

UNITED STATES SENATE

Find Your Senators
Find Your Senators   GO

Search
GO

SENATORS | COMMITTEES | LEGISLATION & RECORDS | ART & HISTORY | VISITORS | REFERENCE

▸ VIRTUAL REFERENCE DESK
▸ VOTES
▸ NOMINATIONS
▸ STATISTICS & LISTS

Women's
History Month

America first
celebrated "Women's
History Week" in
1981, and Congress
later declared March to be
"National
Month"

Oral History Project:
Life in the Senate

Offering a unique perspective on Senate history, the Oral History
Project is a collection of interviews that cover the breadth of the
20th century and now the 21st century. To create this collection,
the Senate historians have interviewed Senate officers,
parliamentarians, clerks, police officers, chiefs of staff,
reporters, photographers, Senate pages, and senators.

▸ 2007 SESSION SCHEDULE
▸ SCHEDULED HEARINGS
▸ ACTIVE LEGISLATION

Floor S
Mond
2:00
cons
pres
Unite

Previous
Thursday

APPROVED WEB SITE

The United States Senate is one of the two houses of the U.S. Congress.
The other is the House of Representatives. You will find comprehensive
information about the **United States Senate** when you visit this Web site.

EDITOR'S CHOICE

the wording on bills. Sometimes majority leaders
return bills to committees for further debate.

Both party leaders have assistants called
whips. They are elected by their party. Whips
count how many votes a bill has from their party
and make sure members are on the floor to vote
on bills. The whips have assistants to help them.
In the 110th Congress, the majority whip was
Richard Durbin of Illinois. The whips of the minority
party, the Republicans, were Mitch McConnell of
Kentucky and Trent Lott of Mississippi.

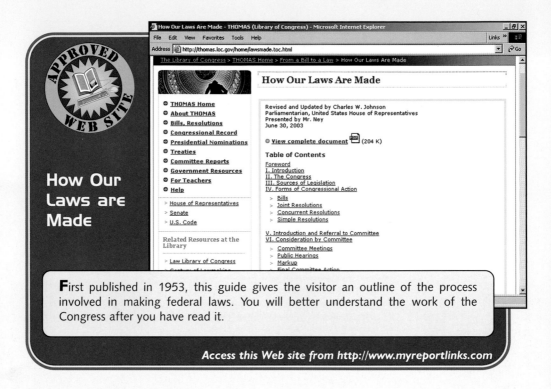

How Our Laws are Made

First published in 1953, this guide gives the visitor an outline of the process involved in making federal laws. You will better understand the work of the Congress after you have read it.

Access this Web site from http://www.myreportlinks.com

➔ MAKING LAWS

The major job of Congress is to pass laws that govern the lives of Americans. During every two-year session, Congress considers close to ten thousand bills. Of these, fewer than one thousand ever become law. Most bills are drawn up by members of Congress. But the ideas for bills come from several sources. One is the congressional members themselves. Another is the president and his advisors.

Bills may be introduced first in either house. The majority, however, begin in the House of Representatives. The Constitution requires that all bills that deal with money, such as paying for federal programs and taxes, begin there. Once both houses come to an agreement and pass the same bill, it is passed on to the president for his approval or rejection.

Proposals for bills are assigned to specific committees for public hearings. Many bills deal with topics that require study by experts. Bills that deal with nuclear energy or military pay, for example, are passed on to the subcommittees for further study.

▲ The House of Representatives uses a type of electronic scoreboard to keep track of votes on the floor.

Debating Bills:
Senate vs. House Procedures

Once a bill is debated thoroughly, the committee decides either to drop the bill or to send it on to the full House or Senate. At this point, the process is different for each chamber. In the House, the bill is read, debated, and read a second time. Amendments are offered to the bill and voted on. Finally, the House votes on the bill. Many bills fail to get a majority vote and are no longer considered. Others are sent back to committees for more debate and rewriting. If the committee sends the revised bill back to the full House, a new vote can be taken. If a majority approves, the bill is passed on to the Senate.

The Senate also has committees to study, debate, and decide if a bill should go on to the full membership for a vote. But unlike the House, the Senate can decide to call for a voice vote on the bill at once. These bills are likely to pass without much discussion. Most bills require more debate. These bills are entered on a calendar for future consideration.

Once the bill comes up for debate, the Senate allows each senator to speak for five minutes. Then amendments can be proposed. If one member objects to the bill, senators may speak for as long as they wish. Senators who object strongly may decide to filibuster the bill.

They will speak for many hours to try to kill the bill.

→ FILIBUSTERS

The filibuster is more typical of modern times than of the past. In the nineteenth century, only sixteen filibusters were made. In the twentieth century, there were more than 260 filibusters. The record for longest time speaking is held by the late Strom Thurmond, a Republican from South Carolina. In 1957, the senator held up vote on a civil rights bill by talking for more than twenty-four hours.

In 1988, the Senate was trying to pass a bill to change how political campaigns were financed. Senators Mitch McConnell, a Republican from Kentucky, and Robert Dole, a Republican from Kansas, opposed the bill and began a filibuster. Majority Leader Robert Byrd, Democrat from West Virginia, ordered that the sergeant at arms arrest Republicans who refused to return to the floor to vote. Senator Bob Packwood, Republican from Oregon, was arrested in his office "and carried feet first into the chamber by three police officers."[5] Byrd was unable to end the filibuster, so the bill was dropped.

If the majority wants to stop the filibuster, sixty of the one hundred senators can vote to limit the time of the filibuster. Then the bill will go before the entire Senate for a vote.

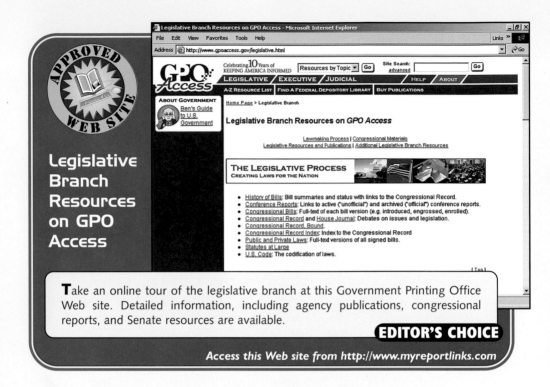

Legislative Branch Resources on GPO Access

Take an online tour of the legislative branch at this Government Printing Office Web site. Detailed information, including agency publications, congressional reports, and Senate resources are available.

EDITOR'S CHOICE

Access this Web site from http://www.myreportlinks.com

⊕CONFERENCE AND COMPROMISE

Almost all bills passed by the House and Senate have different wording. In this case, selected members of both houses meet as a congressional conference committee. They are not allowed to make new proposals. Their task is to work out the differences in the bill.

A bill can die in conference if the members do not agree to a compromise. But usually a bill that goes to conference is considered too important to abandon. Members try hard to give and take, so they send the revised bill to each house for a new vote. The House and Senate follow the same procedure as before. Usually both houses approve of the revised bill. At this point, the bill is sent on to the president for his signature.

THE PRESIDENT'S ACTIONS

If the president signs a bill within ten days, it becomes law. If the president fails to sign the bill within ten days, the bill still becomes law if Congress is in session. If Congress has adjourned during the ten days, the bill is rejected. This is called a pocket veto. If the president is strongly opposed to the bill, he can veto the bill. A veto sends the bill back to Congress.

A president's veto usually kills the bill. Sometimes the president will promise to sign the bill if Congress makes certain changes. The bill then will likely go to committees for rewriting and a vote by both houses. If members of both houses believe they have strong support for the bill, they will meet again for a vote. With a two-thirds approval vote in both houses, the bill becomes law over the president's veto.

INFLUENCES ON MEMBERS OF CONGRESS

The president is an important influence on how members of Congress vote. Members of the president's political party are normally expected to support his policies. The president offers his plans each January in the address to the Congress called the State of the Union address.

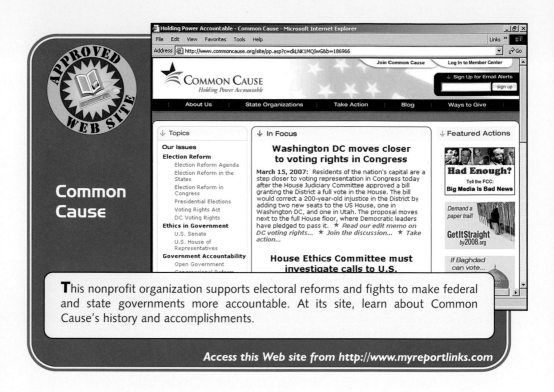

This nonprofit organization supports electoral reforms and fights to make federal and state governments more accountable. At its site, learn about Common Cause's history and accomplishments.

Access this Web site from http://www.myreportlinks.com

The members of the opposing party often disagree with the president's policy program. They will try to convince their supporters that they have a better plan than the president's. But if the president is popular with the voters, the party out of power feels it is necessary to show support for the president.

Almost all members of Congress belong to either the Democratic or Republican parties. So they generally support their own party's program. Party programs are usually determined by the top leaders who consult with party members. On the floor of the House and Senate party leaders apply great pressure on members to support party programs.

→LOBBYISTS AND SPECIAL INTEREST GROUPS

Lobbyists have a major impact on how Congress votes on bills. Lobbyists represent special interest groups from all parts of American life. They range from national corporations and health care companies to labor unions and civil rights groups.

Some lobbyists represent citizens concerned about constitutional rights. One of these is the National Rifle Association, which wants to protect the right to own guns. Another is Common Cause, which supports reforms in government ethics and election reform. Other powerful lobby groups represent senior citizens and people with disabilities.

Lobby groups can present results of extensive research about an issue. This can save members of Congress much time and work. However, many lobby groups contribute money to people who are running for office. When a person wins a seat in Congress, then the lobby group expects that person to promote bills favorable to the lobby group.

Similar to lobbyists, "grass roots" groups send people to Washington to inform Congress of special issues. Environmental groups, for example, exist at local, state, regional, and national levels. Some want to protect forests. Others seek to restrict oil drilling off the shores of populated or ecologically sensitive areas. In recent years, a group that promotes alternative fuels for automobiles has grown stronger.

→THE MEDIA AND THE PUBLIC

Members of Congress need to get their ideas out to the public. The most effective way to present

▲ This image shows all one hundred senators who served in 2003. Senators understand the importance of the camera. Now that C-Span broadcasts all Senate and House hearings, representatives need the camera time to stay in the spotlight.

their programs is through the media. Rutgers University professor Ross Baker writes, "[I]t is journalists—above all others—who tell the story of Congress and its members to the world."[6]

Some members of Congress appear before the media almost daily. Front-page headlines in print and lead stories on television inform the public about what is going on in government. Politicians realize that public opinion is the most important influence on Congress. In 1979, the House allowed a cable television news network, C-SPAN, to broadcast all of its proceedings. In 1986, C-SPAN began televising the proceedings in the Senate.

3 HISTORY OF THE LEGISLATIVE BRANCH

The roots of today's Congress go back to the American Revolution. Fifty-six men from twelve of the thirteen colonies met in Philadelphia in the fall of 1774. This was the First Continental Congress. They called for the British government to respect the colonists' rights as Englishmen.

They were unhappy with the British response. So they met again in 1775. After a year of debate, fifty-five men at this Second Continental Congress signed the Declaration of Independence in 1776. The document describes the abuses by the king of Great Britain. Then the Declaration proclaims "That these United Colonies are, . . . Free and Independent States."[1]

The states were united after the American Revolution. But the central government was weak.

Each state controlled its own money, trade, and army. Many state leaders wanted a stronger central government. They called for a Constitutional Convention to be held in Philadelphia in February 1787.

⇨CONSTITUTIONAL CONVENTION

For seven months, state representatives worked on a plan for governing the United States. They created the modern Congress of two houses. The "lower house," called the House of Representatives, was based on population. And the "upper house," called the Senate, was made up of two senators from each state.

Debates over other issues took up more time. Exhausted from the long spring and summer of work, on September 17, 1787, thirty-nine men from thirteen states signed the final draft of the Constitution.

By June 1788, nine states had approved, or ratified, the Constitution. It became the basic law of the nation. The first ten amendments, or Bill of Rights, were proposed in September 1789. Within two years, the amendments had been approved by the states. The work of the last Continental Congress was finished. It had created a federal government with a strong legislature that survives more than two hundred years later.

The **Continental Congress Broadside Collection** (256 titles) and the **Constitutional Convention Broadside Collection** (21 titles) contain 277 documents relating to the work of Congress and the drafting and ratification of the Constitution. Items include extracts of the journals of Congress, resolutions, proclamations, committee reports, treaties, and early printed versions of the United States Constitution and the Declaration of Independence. Most

At least 277 documents that relate to the Continental Congress are available on the **Documents from the Continental Congress and the Constitutional Convention** site. Also included are archival copies of the United States Constitution and the Declaration of Independence, committee reports, treaties, and broadsides.

EDITOR'S CHOICE

➡ POLITICAL PARTIES

The early sessions of Congress were served by skilled politicians. Most of them had served in the Continental Congresses or in their state governments. Many of them attended the Constitutional Convention. But these men had differing views about how strong the federal government should be.

These divisions were clear. Virginia Senator John Taylor wrote: "The existence of two parties in Congress is apparent. The fact is disclosed almost upon every important question. . . . [from issues of] war or peace—navigation or commerce."[2]

One party was called the Federalists. They believed in a strong central government. They planned for the government to help develop the nation's economy. Alexander Hamilton was their leader. They were opposed by the Democratic-Republicans. They were led by Thomas Jefferson and James Madison. The Democratic-Republicans felt that most laws should be decided at the state and local levels.

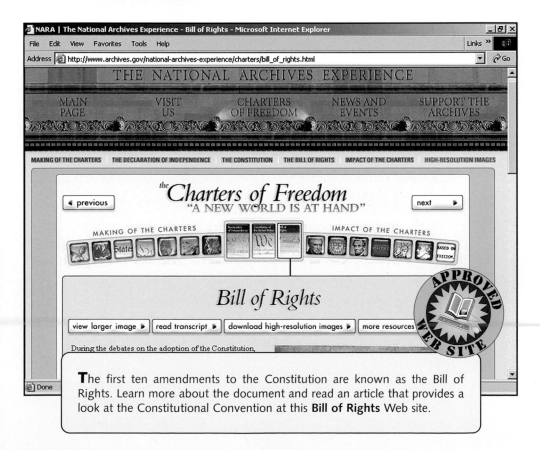

The first ten amendments to the Constitution are known as the Bill of Rights. Learn more about the document and read an article that provides a look at the Constitutional Convention at this **Bill of Rights** Web site.

→SLAVERY AND TERRITORIAL EXPANSION

At the Constitutional Convention, a compromise had saved the Constitution. The Southern states would not agree to get rid of slavery. So the delegates agreed to count slaves as three fifths of a person to figure representation and taxes. Fifteen years later, the Louisiana Purchase opened up new land for settlers. In the future, these settlers formed governments that became states.

Congressmen from the South insisted that slavery be allowed in the new states. But most people in Northern states wanted to stop the spread of slavery. Across the nation, people argued about the issue of slavery. In Congress, Daniel Webster, Henry Clay, and John C. Calhoun became national figures from these debates.

→MISSOURI COMPROMISE OF 1820

Missouri applied for statehood in 1819. At the time, there were eleven slave and eleven free states in the Senate. The House, though, had 105 members from free states and 81 from slave states.

The House voted 87 to 76 to admit Missouri on two conditions: It had to ban slaves from entering the state. And it had to agree to gradual emancipation (freedom of slaves). All the congressmen from the South voted against the bill. The Senate rejected much of the bill, so the issue was left unsettled.

Henry Clay was a member of the Whig Party and an advocate for the abolition of slavery. Details of his life can be found on the Web site of **Ashland: The Henry Clay Estate.**

Maine had petitioned for statehood as a free state. Speaker Henry Clay declared that Maine would be allowed statehood only if Missouri was admitted as a slave state. The Senate passed a similar bill. Part of the Senate bill outlawed slavery in the land of the Louisiana Purchase north of 36°30' north latitude. The Senate passed the bill, but the House rejected it.

From all around Washington, D.C., people came to listen to the debate. There was talk of secession or war. Then on March 1, 1820, Henry

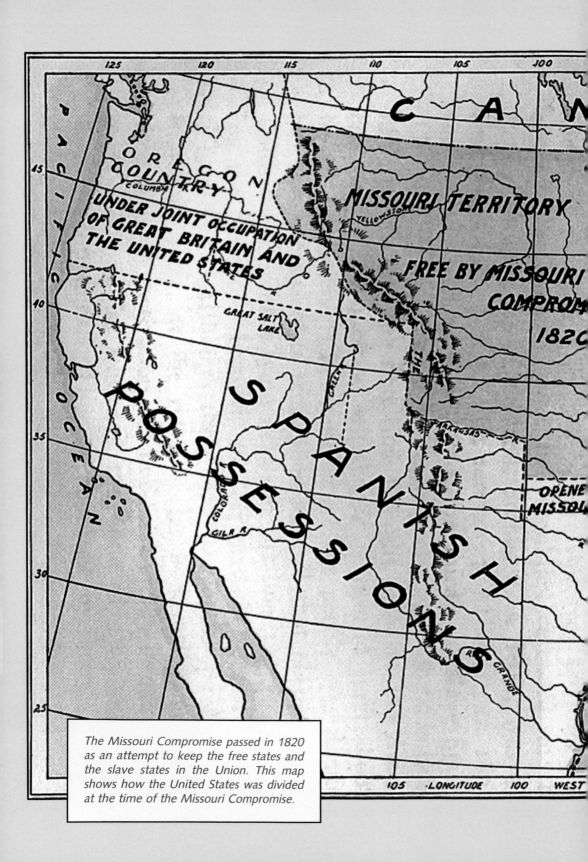

The Missouri Compromise passed in 1820 as an attempt to keep the free states and the slave states in the Union. This map shows how the United States was divided at the time of the Missouri Compromise.

Clay worked out a compromise. Two bills were passed. One admitted Maine as a free state. The other allowed Missouri to enter with no ban on slavery. The second bill also outlawed slavery north of 36°30′ latitude.

⊙CONGRESS AND THE NULLIFICATION ISSUE

Almost all main disputes in Congress before the Civil War involved slavery. One of these clashes was whether states could reject a federal law.

Congress passed a high tariff in 1828. A tariff is a tax on imported goods. People would have to pay more for products made overseas. So, they would buy American-made goods because they were cheaper. The result would stimulate new industry. The American economy would grow faster.

Leaders in the South opposed a high tariff. Increased tariffs meant paying higher prices for supplies. But the South had a minority in Congress. So they decided they could nullify, or reject, federal laws. If Congress disagreed, the South would secede from the United States.

John C. Calhoun of South Carolina led the argument for the South. He claimed that the states created the federal government. Therefore, the states could determine whether a law was constitutional.

The North, on the other hand, felt that the Constitution was a contract with the American

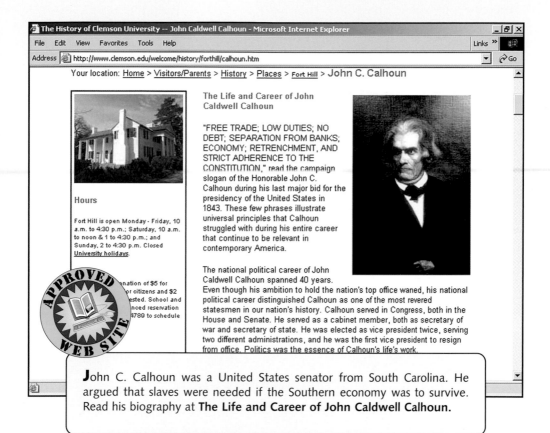

The History of Clemson University -- John Caldwell Calhoun - Microsoft Internet Explorer

File   Edit   View   Favorites   Tools   Help   Links »

Address http://www.clemson.edu/welcome/history/forthill/calhoun.htm   Go

Your location: Home > Visitors/Parents > History > Places > Fort Hill > John C. Calhoun

The Life and Career of John Caldwell Calhoun

"FREE TRADE; LOW DUTIES; NO DEBT; SEPARATION FROM BANKS; ECONOMY; RETRENCHMENT, AND STRICT ADHERENCE TO THE CONSTITUTION," read the campaign slogan of the Honorable John C. Calhoun during his last major bid for the presidency of the United States in 1843. These few phrases illustrate universal principles that Calhoun struggled with during his entire career that continue to be relevant in contemporary America.

Hours

Fort Hill is open Monday - Friday, 10 a.m. to 4:30 p.m.; Saturday, 10 a.m. to noon & 1 to 4:30 p.m.; and Sunday, 2 to 4:30 p.m. Closed University holidays.

The national political career of John Caldwell Calhoun spanned 40 years. Even though his ambition to hold the nation's top office waned, his national political career distinguished Calhoun as one of the most revered statesmen in our nation's history. Calhoun served in Congress, both in the House and Senate. He served as a cabinet member, both as secretary of war and secretary of state. He was elected as vice president twice, serving two different administrations, and he was the first vice president to resign from office. Politics was the essence of Calhoun's life's work.

...nation of $5 for ...r citizens and $2 ...ested. School and ...nced reservation ...4789 to schedule

APPROVED WEB SITE

John C. Calhoun was a United States senator from South Carolina. He argued that slaves were needed if the Southern economy was to survive. Read his biography at **The Life and Career of John Caldwell Calhoun.**

people, not separate states. Therefore, no state had a right to nullify a federal law.

In November 1832, South Carolina declared the federal tariff laws null and void. The state leaders said that the tariffs would not be collected. If the federal government interfered, South Carolina would withdraw from the Union.

President Andrew Jackson threatened to send in troops to enforce the law. However, Senator Henry Clay worked tirelessly with Calhoun on a compromise. Congress lowered tariffs over the next ten years to a level approved by the South.

→FINAL ATTEMPTS TO SETTLE THE SLAVERY ISSUE

In 1849, California asked to become a state. Slavery would be barred. Most people agreed that New Mexico and Utah would soon enter the Union. They were also likely to forbid slavery. Mississippi Senator Jefferson Davis said, "For the first time, we are about permanently to destroy the balance of power between the sections."[3]

The South was also angry that the North had ignored the Fugitive Slave Law of 1793. Many people in the North refused to help Southerners capture their runaway slaves. Many Northerners believed that slavery and the slave trade should also be banned in the nation's capital.

The debate in the Senate over these issues is "the most famous congressional debate in U.S. history."[4] Henry Clay, seventy-two years old, offered a compromise. Sixty-eight-year-old Senator Daniel Webster of Massachusetts opposed slavery. But he proposed a compromise on the Fugitive Slave Law and the slave trade in Washington, D.C.

Sixty-eight-year-old John Calhoun was so sick he had to ask a colleague to read his speech. Calhoun believed that the Union could not survive. He recommended an amendment to the Constitution. He proposed two presidents, one from the North and one from the South. Furthermore, the

North must agree to enforce slave laws and give the South equal rights in the territories. Otherwise, the South would withdraw peacefully from the Union.

Clay's compromise was firmly denounced by New York Senator William Seward. He appealed to a "higher law than the Constitution."[5] After six months of bitter debate, a new senator suggested a way to settle the impasse. Stephen A. Douglas, Democrat from Illinois, broke Clay's proposals into smaller issues. Congress passed most of Douglas's proposals. California was admitted as a free state. New Mexico and Utah were allowed to determine the status of slavery on their own.

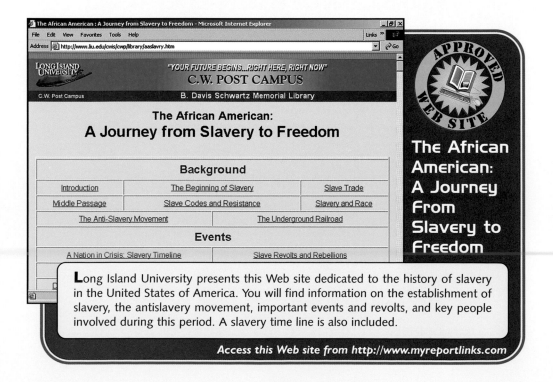

The African American : A Journey from Slavery to Freedom - Microsoft Internet Explorer

File   Edit   View   Favorites   Tools   Help   Links »

Address http://www.liu.edu/cwis/cwp/library/aaslavry.htm   Go

LONG ISLAND UNIVERSITY

"YOUR FUTURE BEGINS...RIGHT HERE, RIGHT NOW"
C.W. POST CAMPUS

C.W. Post Campus   B. Davis Schwartz Memorial Library

The African American:
A Journey from Slavery to Freedom

Background

Introduction	The Beginning of Slavery	Slave Trade
Middle Passage	Slave Codes and Resistance	Slavery and Race
The Anti-Slavery Movement		The Underground Railroad

Events

| A Nation in Crisis: Slavery Timeline | Slave Revolts and Rebellions |

The African American: A Journey From Slavery to Freedom

Long Island University presents this Web site dedicated to the history of slavery in the United States of America. You will find information on the establishment of slavery, the antislavery movement, important events and revolts, and key people involved during this period. A slavery time line is also included.

Access this Web site from http://www.myreportlinks.com

The slave trade in Washington, D.C., was outlawed, but not slavery. And the Fugitive Slave Law was revised to make it easier to enforce.

➡CONGRESS TAKES CONTROL

In the end, nothing worked to hold the nation together. Antislavery forces were upset with compromises to satisfy the South. They united to form the Republican party. Abraham Lincoln was their second presidential nominee. He was elected president on November 6, 1860.

Lincoln was assassinated in 1865, and Andrew Johnson took over as president. He planned to allow states back into the Union under two conditions: First of all, they had to abolish slavery. Secondly, they had to pledge loyalty to the United States. Slavery was formally abolished by the Thirteenth Amendment. However, Republicans in Congress wanted to punish the South for its rebellion.

When it met in December 1865, Congress took control of Reconstruction. The Republicans were led by Senator Charles Sumner of Massachusetts and Representative Thaddeus Stevens of Pennsylvania. Congress rejected all representatives and senators sent by Southern states.

➡RECONSTRUCTION

Congress also passed the majority of its Reconstruction program over President Johnson's veto.

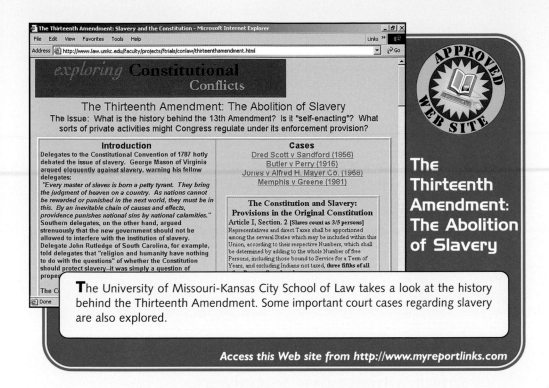

The Thirteenth Amendment: Slavery and the Constitution - Microsoft Internet Explorer

File Edit View Favorites Tools Help   Links »

Address http://www.law.umkc.edu/faculty/projects/ftrials/conlaw/thirteenthamendment.html   Go

exploring **Constitutional**
Conflicts

The Thirteenth Amendment: The Abolition of Slavery

The Issue: What is the history behind the 13th Amendment? Is it "self-enacting"? What sorts of private activities might Congress regulate under its enforcement provision?

Introduction

Delegates to the Constitutional Convention of 1787 hotly debated the issue of slavery. George Mason of Virginia argued eloquently against slavery, warning his fellow delegates:
"Every master of slaves is born a petty tyrant. They bring the judgment of heaven on a country. As nations cannot be rewarded or punished in the next world, they must be in this. By an inevitable chain of causes and effects, providence punishes national sins by national calamities." Southern delegates, on the other hand, argued strenuously that the new government should not be allowed to interfere with the institution of slavery. Delegate John Rutledge of South Carolina, for example, told delegates that "religion and humanity have nothing to do with the questions" of whether the Constitution should protect slavery--it was simply a question of proper

Cases

Dred Scott v Sandford (1856)
Butler v Perry (1916)
Jones v Alfred H. Mayer Co. (1968)
Memphis v Greene (1981)

The Constitution and Slavery:
Provisions in the Original Constitution

Article I, Section. 2 [Slaves count as 3/5 persons]
Representatives and direct Taxes shall be apportioned among the several States which may be included within this Union, according to their respective Numbers, which shall be determined by adding to the whole Number of free Persons, including those bound to Service for a Term of Years, and excluding Indians not taxed, **three fifths of all**

APPROVED WEB SITE

The Thirteenth Amendment: The Abolition of Slavery

The University of Missouri-Kansas City School of Law takes a look at the history behind the Thirteenth Amendment. Some important court cases regarding slavery are also explored.

Access this Web site from http://www.myreportlinks.com

The United States' first Civil Rights Act was passed in 1866 over Johnson's veto. The law stated that African Americans (but not American Indians) were now citizens of the United States. They had the same rights as any other citizen. If necessary, the federal government would use force to enforce their rights.

Congress then passed the Fourteenth Amendment in 1868. This amendment states that American citizens are people born in the United States or naturalized. It goes on to say that all citizens have equal rights. Furthermore, these rights will be protected by the government.

In March 1867, over another Johnson veto, Congress passed the Military Reconstruction Act. Ten of the former Confederate states were divided into five military districts. The overall command of the Reconstruction areas was given to Civil War hero and Republican General Ulysses S. Grant. The act also specified the requirements states had to meet to be readmitted to the union.

Then, in 1870 Congress passed the Fifteenth Amendment. This guaranteed the right to vote to African Americans. By this time, all of the former Confederate states had been readmitted to the Union.

IMPEACHMENT OF PRESIDENT ANDREW JOHNSON

In its conflict with President Johnson, Congress took the position that the president's duty was to execute the laws. It was Congress's job to make the laws. This battle climaxed with the House's impeachment of the president in 1868.

Congress had passed the Tenure of Office Act in 1867. Many officials appointed by the president need Senate approval. This law said the president could not fire these officials without the Senate's consent. Johnson fired Edwin Stanton, the secretary of war. With Congress's support, Stanton refused to leave.

The House of Representatives charged Johnson with breaking the law and impeached him. But the Senate failed by one vote to convict him. By charging the president, "the radical Republicans . . . effectively asserted the dominance of Congress in the federal government."[6]

⮕ GROUNDWORK FOR THE MODERN CONGRESS

In the 1870s, the United States began a period of rapid industrial growth. Railroads expanded across the continent. New banks opened to help finance industries. From steel plants and coal mines to food processing and publishing, the United States economy grew rapidly.

Much of the economic growth involved some action from Congress. From 1871 to 1881, about thirty-seven thousand bills were introduced to Congress. In 1900 alone, eighty-one thousand bills were introduced. Congress had to expand its number of committees to deal with this huge increase.

⮕ BALANCING POWER IN BOTH CHAMBERS

By this time, party leaders had become very powerful men. In the House, the Speaker was the majority party leader. He controlled which bills to consider and which ones to block. Thomas B. Reed of Maine was the Speaker for most sessions between 1885 and 1899. He controlled legislation so completely that he was nicknamed Czar Reed.

This sketch by artist Theodore R. Davis shows his view of what the scene was like at the Senate impeachment trial of President Andrew Johnson.

A few years later, another Republican speaker, Joseph G. Cannon of Illinois, followed Reed's methods. But in 1910, Republicans and Democrats took away much of the Speaker's power.

The Senate was different. At the time, Senators were named by their state legislatures, not elected by the people. Therefore, they felt little need to satisfy voters. Large corporations gave huge sums of money to senators to influence their vote. Many senators became extremely rich.

The public wanted to have a more direct voice in selecting their senators. After many years of pressure, the Senate passed the Seventeenth Amendment in 1911. The amendment states that each state will have two senators "elected by the people." It was ratified by the states and went into effect in 1913.

➔THE PROGRESSIVE ERA

From 1880 to 1920, Congress passed laws that laid the groundwork for modern America. They were directed at controlling the abuse and injustices created by rapid economic growth. Many of these laws have since been revised and strengthened.

Congress passed the Pendleton Act in 1883. This act protected the jobs of tens of thousands of people who worked for the federal government. The Civil Service Commission was set up to monitor federal appointments and give tests for new jobs.

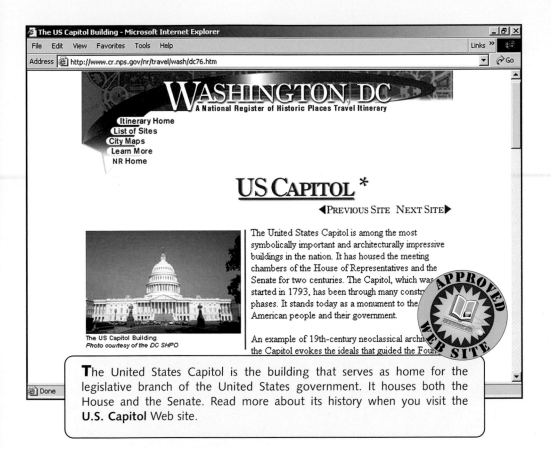

The United States Capitol is the building that serves as home for the legislative branch of the United States government. It houses both the House and the Senate. Read more about its history when you visit the **U.S. Capitol** Web site.

Another reform came out of the Interstate Commerce Act passed in 1887. This act created the Interstate Commerce Commission to control unfair railroad rates. In 1890, the Sherman Anti-Trust Act was passed to regulate the growth of businesses. It was also supposed to prevent unfair business practices. Enforcing these acts proved more difficult. Congress did not want to discourage the growth of big business.

Even more bills aimed at cleaning up abuses in certain industries were enacted in the early

twentieth century. In 1906, Congress passed the
Pure Food and Drug Act and the Meat Inspection
Act. These acts make food, drugs, and meat safer
for consumers. Also, the laws established the
government's right to try to monitor the nation's
economy.

These women are parading in Washington, D.C., on March 3,
1913, in an effort to gain support for women's suffrage, or the
right to vote. The Nineteenth Amendment giving women the
vote was ratified on August 18, 1920.

Until the twentieth century, the government depended on tariffs to raise money. Only during the Civil War had there been an income tax. In 1895, Congress passed a bill creating a national income tax. But the Supreme Court ruled it was illegal because the Constitution said there would

be no direct taxes by the government. Two decades later, the Sixteenth Amendment created the income tax.

The federal law making the deepest impact on American life gave women the right to vote in national elections. In 1918, the Nineteenth Amendment, granting women the right to vote, passed Congress. It became the law of the land in 1920 when two thirds of the states ratified it.

➲ CONGRESS AND FDR

By 1930, the United States was suffering from "the severest and most prolonged economic crisis in its history."[7] This time of suffering became known as the Great Depression. By 1932, many large industries had reduced production. Millions of workers lost their jobs. Unemployment in urban areas rose to 50 percent and higher. Toledo, Ohio, reported an unemployment rate of 80 percent. Banks serving farmers were in trouble because they had loaned out too much money.

At the same time, the Midwest was hit by huge dust storms that continued for several years. Farmers were hit hard by the Depression. They made less money. As a result, they could not pay back their loans. More than one third of American farmers lost their land between 1929 and 1932.

Democrats won control of Congress in 1932. They held the majority in most elections for the next sixty years. Working with Democratic President Franklin D. Roosevelt, Congress passed a series of laws that began to revive the economy. This program is called the New Deal.

The Tennessee Valley Authority was created in 1933. It is a public power company that built a series of dams along the Tennessee River in the southeastern United States. The waterpower from these dams provides electricity to seven states.

Another program passed in 1935 is the Social Security system. This provides help to people who

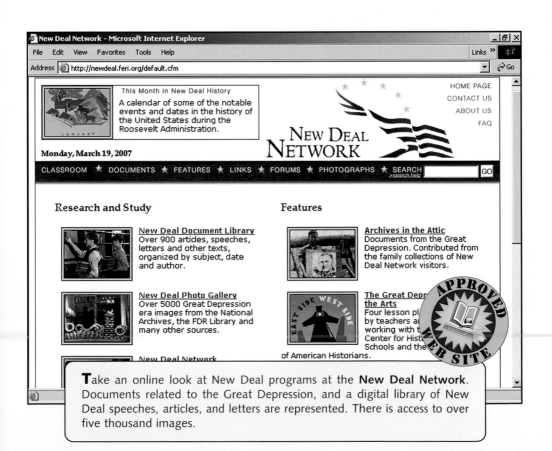

Take an online look at New Deal programs at the **New Deal Network**. Documents related to the Great Depression, and a digital library of New Deal speeches, articles, and letters are represented. There is access to over five thousand images.

lose their jobs. It also assures millions of retired workers that they will receive pensions. Congress also passed the National Labor Relations Act (NLRA). The NLRA gave workers the right to organize labor unions. Another bill created a national minimum wage, the forty-hour work-week, and stricter rules for child labor.

During World War II, Congress worked closely with Roosevelt. They created the Selective Service Administration to supervise the military draft to provide soldiers for the U.S. Army.

→ DEMOCRATS RULE

Republicans tend to be conservative in their beliefs. Conservatives believe that most of the work being done by the federal government should be done at the state level. They also believe that many of the New Deal programs are unconsti-tutional.

Most Democrats, on the other hand, are more liberal in their views. They believe the federal gov-ernment has a duty to encourage business and give help to the people. There are some Democrats who support conservative policies. Most of them represent Southern States. Sometimes they vote with Republicans on bills.

In both parties, there are many members of Congress who consider themselves moderates. These legislators have the ability to work with both conservatives and liberals to work out compromises so that bills can become laws.

Democrats ran Congress most of the time from 1933 to 1995. Liberal Democrats were able to work with moderates for civil rights laws in the 1950s. Under the strong leadership of Senate Majority Leader Lyndon Johnson, Congress passed a Civil Rights Act in 1957. Although this legislation was not very significant, it did create the Commission on Civil Rights. It also gave the attorney general of the United States the right to go to court to enforce voting rights.

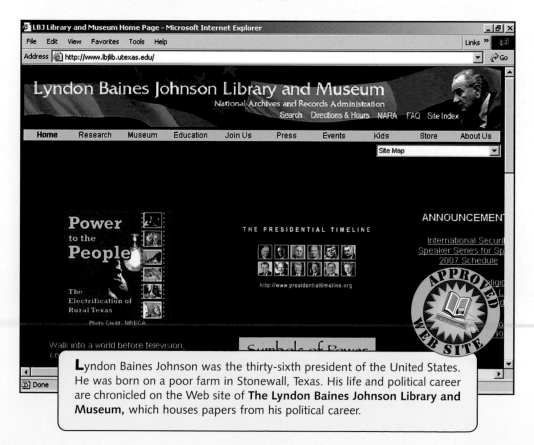

Lyndon Baines Johnson was the thirty-sixth president of the United States. He was born on a poor farm in Stonewall, Texas. His life and political career are chronicled on the Web site of **The Lyndon Baines Johnson Library and Museum,** which houses papers from his political career.

In the 1960s and 1970s, the Vietnam War was a major issue in Congress and throughout the United States. These soldiers are moving away from a napalm strike during 1966.

In 1964, after Johnson had become president, Congress passed a second Civil Rights Act. This act guaranteed equal access for all people to public facilities such as parks, hotels, and restaurants. The act also promised equal job opportunities to all races. In 1965, Congress added a Voting Rights Act that increased registered African-American voters in the South by five hundred thousand. These programs were known as the Great Society, and many were very controversial at that time.

Congress also worked with President Johnson to pass major bills that are still improving the lives of many Americans. The bills include Medicare, programs to help the poor, and increased aid for education.

WAR POWERS ACT

The major issue Dividing Congress and the nation in the 1960s and 1970s was the Vietnam War (1961–75). Congress usually gave presidents Lyndon B. Johnson and Richard Nixon what they asked for to fight the war. (Nixon was elected in part because he promised to end the war.) But as the war stretched on, Congress became more impatient with Nixon's leadership. In 1973, Congress passed the War Powers Act. This bill requires presidents to get Congress's approval for any plan to send troops somewhere to fight.

During Nixon's second term, the press revealed that he and some of his advisors had covered up crimes related to a robbery at the Democratic party headquarters in the Watergate Hotel. The House Judiciary Committee voted to impeach (charge) Nixon in July 1974. Soon after, Nixon resigned. Former Republican Minority Leader Gerald R. Ford of Michigan, then vice president, took over the presidency. However, Congress remained Democratic.

→ REPUBLICAN REVIVAL

In 1981, Republican California governor Ronald Reagan became president. The Republicans also won the majority of seats in the Senate for the first time in twenty-eight years. The House remained Democratic, although they lost thirty-three seats. Many of the Democrats' losses were in the South, where voters were switching to the Republican party.

Power in Congress was split between the two parties. Conservative Democrats often voted with Republicans and passed Reagan's proposals. They reduced taxes and spending for programs in the United States, and increased defense spending. By the mid-1980s, the population of the South and the West was growing rapidly. This increase in population gave these regions more seats in the House.

Except for California, voters in these regions tend to be more conservative than voters in the North and East. Therefore, they have been electing more Republicans to Congress. As a result, Republican political power climbed in the late 1980s. Their successes changed Congress in 1995.

Georgia's Congressman Newt Gingrich guided Republicans to victory in 1994. They took control of both the Senate and House in 1995. Except

House Speaker Nancy Pelosi addresses the press during a news conference on March 13, 2007. Standing behind her left to right are Representative Rahm Emanuel from Illinois, House Majority Whip James Clyburn of South Carolina, and House Majority Leader Steny Hoyer of Maryland.

for the 107th Congress (2001–03), Republicans held the majority through the 109th Congress (2005–06).

In the first decade of the twenty-first century, many critics claim that Congress is no longer strong. They say that the Republican majority simply follows the lead of Republican president George W. Bush.

In 2005, the public's trust in the President began to drop. Members of both parties began asking the President for plans to withdraw troops from Iraq. Congress also questioned Bush's surveillance programs. Democrats, especially, have called for investigations to decide if the President has acted illegally in his plans to fight terrorism. The 110th Congress (2007) was controlled by the Democrats.

This struggle for power between presidents and Congress is a major theme in American history.

4 POWERFUL PERSONS WHO HAVE SERVED

Congress has been well served by Americans from all walks of life. People from the most common backgrounds can be elected to state and federal office. Through 2007, twenty-two of the forty-three presidents have served in Congress. Eight of them served in both the House and Senate.

In the post-World War II period, six of the ten presidents served in one or both of the houses of Congress. Harry S Truman served in the Senate. Both George H. W. Bush and Gerald R. Ford served in the House. John F. Kennedy, Lyndon Johnson, and Richard M. Nixon served in both branches of the legislature.

In 1959, the Senate unveiled portraits of five renowned members from the past. Three were from the nineteenth century. They were South Carolina's John C. Calhoun, Kentucky's Henry Clay, and Massachusetts' Daniel Webster. Two of them were from the twentieth century: Wisconsin's Robert M. La Follette, Sr., and Ohio's Robert A. Taft. In September 2004, two more portraits were added to the display in the Senate Reception Room. They were Michigan's Arthur H. Vandenberg and New York's Robert F. Wagner. More selections will be added in the future.

➔THE GREAT TRIUMVIRATE

From 1810 to 1850, John Calhoun, Henry Clay, and Daniel Webster had a major impact on

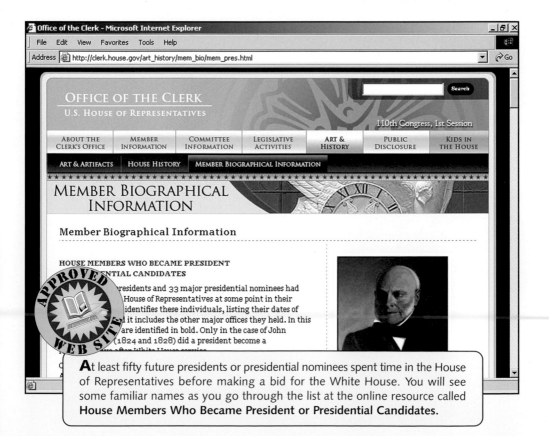

At least fifty future presidents or presidential nominees spent time in the House of Representatives before making a bid for the White House. You will see some familiar names as you go through the list at the online resource called **House Members Who Became President or Presidential Candidates.**

American politics. All three served in the Senate and the House of Representatives. And each of them served in a president's Cabinet as secretary of state during this period. Newspaper editors nicknamed them the Great Triumvirate.

For almost two decades, Calhoun defended the Southern way of life in the Senate. He argued that slavery was a vital part of the Southern economy. He also maintained that states had the right not to obey a federal law.

→ CALHOUN

Calhoun was determined to stop the Compromise of 1850. But he was so sick he had to be carried onto the Senate floor. His close friend, Senator John Mason of Virginia, read his speech for him. Just before he died, Calhoun wrote Mason that "The Union is doomed" no matter what the decision on the compromise. He predicted that the nation would split up "within twelve years or three presidential terms. . . . [and likely] explode in a presidential election."[1]

Calhoun did not live to see how close he was to being correct. He was sixty-eight when he died from tuberculosis on March 31, 1850. Eleven years later, the Civil War began when federal troops fired on Fort Sumter, South Carolina, on April 12, 1861.

John C. Calhoun warned early on that the Union would dissolve. He died in 1850, eleven years before the outbreak of the Civil War.

→CLAY—THE GREAT COMPROMISER

Calhoun's rival Henry Clay was seventy-three when he worked out the terms of the Compromise of 1850. He had built his reputation first as Speaker of the House. Before he became a senator, many people already thought of Clay as the second most powerful man in the nation, aside from the president.[2]

Clay's American Plan promoted the spread of canals and highways, a strong military, and protection for American industries. As Speaker, Clay worked constantly to bring together different sides of an issue, a skill that earned him the nickname the Great Compromiser.

Clay became a senator in 1831. The discord between the North and South was becoming more intense. Clay believed that the Union should be saved at any cost. In the 1850 debate over slavery, Clay worked tirelessly to get both sides to compromise. But like Calhoun, Clay was very sick with tuberculosis. The time had come for younger men to work out the details of the Compromise of 1850. Clay died on June 29, 1852.

→WEBSTER CALLS FOR "LIBERTY AND UNION"

Daniel Webster was the third member of the Great Triumvirate. He entered the Senate in 1827. By that time, Webster was already famous for his dramatic speaking style. His speech on January 26, 1830, has become legendary. In defense of national unity, he declared, "Liberty and Union, now and forever, one and inseparable."[3]

Webster was opposed to slavery. However, in the 1850 Senate debate, he insisted that the North bargain with the South to save the Union. Moderates in the nation praised him. Those who believed that slavery was evil condemned him. In July 1850, Webster resigned and was named secretary of state. He was seventy on October 24, 1852, when he died after being thrown from his horse.

➲CZAR REED

At the end of the Civil War there were 36 million people in America. By 1900, the population had reached 76 million. This growth created dozens of new openings in the House. The number of bills passing through the House increased rapidly.

Thomas B. Reed, a Republican from Maine, became Speaker of the House in 1889. He set up new rules that gave the Speaker more control over legislation. Democrats in the House often refused to answer roll calls for a vote. Instead of closing down the Senate, Reed simply declared them present. Therefore, the House had enough members present to vote on bills. When his opponents tried to leave the room, Reed had the doors locked. His strongarm methods earned him the nickname Czar Reed.

Thomas "Czar" Reed was the strong-willed Speaker of the House who held the post from 1889 to 1891, and again from 1895 until 1899.

⊖"Uncle Joe" Cannon

In 1903, Illinois Republican Joseph Cannon was elected Speaker. He is often ranked as the most powerful Speaker in history. A small man, Cannon wore a long, stringy beard. He was always smoking a "well-chewed cigar." Whenever he spoke, he was "humorous, profane, [and] ungrammatical."[4] People liked Cannon and called him "Uncle Joe." The first legislative office building, separate from the Capitol, opened in 1906 and was named after him.

In 1909 he lost the Speaker's position. But the voters keep electing him to return to the House. He served a total of forty-seven years. When Cannon retired on March 3, 1923, his photograph appeared on the cover of the first issue of *Time* magazine.

⊖"Mista Sam" Rayburn

The most recently built office building for House members opened in 1965. It was named after Sam Rayburn, Democrat from Texas. Between 1940 and 1961, he held the speaker's post for seventeen years. He entered the House in 1913. Over his long career, Rayburn earned the respect of everyone for his fairness. He won over members to his side by friendly discussions in private. He worked to build consensus, saying, "A jackass can kick a barn down, but it takes a carpenter to build one."[5]

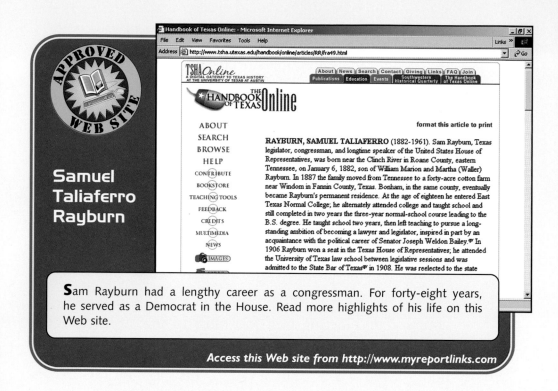

Handbook of Texas Online: - Microsoft Internet Explorer

File Edit View Favorites Tools Help   Links »

Address 🔗 http://www.tsha.utexas.edu/handbook/online/articles/RR/fra49.html   ⮎ Go

TSHA *Online*
A DIGITAL GATEWAY TO TEXAS HISTORY
AT THE UNIVERSITY OF TEXAS AT AUSTIN

About · News · Search · Contact · Giving · Links · FAQ · Join
Publications · Education · Events · Southwestern Historical Quarterly · The Handbook of Texas Online

THE HANDBOOK OF TEXAS *Online*

ABOUT
SEARCH
BROWSE
HELP
CONTRIBUTE
BOOKSTORE
TEACHING TOOLS
FEEDBACK
CREDITS
MULTIMEDIA
NEWS
IMAGES

format this article to print

RAYBURN, SAMUEL TALIAFERRO (1882-1961). Sam Rayburn, Texas legislator, congressman, and longtime speaker of the United States House of Representatives, was born near the Clinch River in Roane County, eastern Tennessee, on January 6, 1882, son of William Marion and Martha (Waller) Rayburn. In 1887 the family moved from Tennessee to a forty-acre cotton farm near Windom in Fannin County, Texas. Bonham, in the same county, eventually became Rayburn's permanent residence. At the age of eighteen he entered East Texas Normal College; he alternately attended college and taught school and still completed in two years the three-year normal-school course leading to the B.S. degree. He taught school two years, then left teaching to pursue a longstanding ambition of becoming a lawyer and legislator, inspired in part by an acquaintance with the political career of Senator Joseph Weldon Bailey. In 1906 Rayburn won a seat in the Texas House of Representatives; he attended the University of Texas law school between legislative sessions and was admitted to the State Bar of Texas in 1908. He was reelected to the state

Samuel Taliaferro Rayburn

Sam Rayburn had a lengthy career as a congressman. For forty-eight years, he served as a Democrat in the House. Read more highlights of his life on this Web site.

Access this Web site from http://www.myreportlinks.com

Rayburn backed President Franklin Roosevelt's New Deal programs in the 1930s. Later on, he helped win support for civil rights bills in the 1950s. Rayburn's reputation for honesty was solid. He refused to accept money from special interest groups. Most of his colleagues liked and respected him so much they addressed him as "Mista Sam."

➔THE JOHNSON TREATMENT

Lyndon B. Johnson learned politics from his friend Sam Rayburn. Johnson served in the House from 1937 to 1948. He was elected to the Senate in 1948. Within a couple of years he had become a powerful leader.

For most of the 1950s, Lyndon Johnson was the majority leader in the Senate. His methods of persuasion were called "the Johnson Treatment." Reporters Rowland Evans and Robert Novak wrote: "He [Johnson] moved in close, his face a scant millimeter from his target, his eyes widening and narrowing, his eyebrows rising and falling. From his pockets poured clippings, memos, statistics. Mimicry, humor, and genius of analogy made The Treatment an almost hypnotic experience and rendered the target stunned and helpless."[6]

Johnson sponsored civil rights bills in the 1950s. But his fellow Democrats from the South often resisted. When he became president, Johnson applied the Johnson Treatment to Congress and got a strong civil rights bill passed. In many ways, he was still "majority leader" of his party even while president.

➲ WAR HEROES: INOUYE AND McCAIN

Senator Daniel K. Inouye, a Democrat from Hawaii, was only nineteen years old when he joined the Army in 1943. He returned from World War II with the Bronze Star Medal, awarded for heroic deeds in battle. Years later, he was presented with the Medal of Honor for his bravery in the European campaign. Inouye holds the record for the longest service of any Asian American serving in Congress. He began as Hawaii's first

▲ Senator John McCain (right) meets with President Ronald Reagan. A former war hero, McCain is one of the most respected senators in Congress.

member of the House in 1959. Then he won a seat in the Senate in 1963.

A generation younger than Inouye, Senator John McCain fought for his country in Vietnam. He has become a major spokesman for the Republican party. McCain graduated from the Naval Academy in 1958. While serving as a pilot in the Vietnam War, he was shot down over Hanoi. He parachuted from his plane, but broke both arms and legs when he landed. He still is unable to raise his arms above his head. McCain spent five-and-a-half years as a prisoner of war in North Vietnam. He spent more than two of those years confined alone in a six-foot by nine-foot hole in the ground.

After his release in 1973, McCain received many honors. Among them were the Silver Star, Bronze Star, Legion of Merit, Purple Heart, and Distinguished Flying Cross. The nation admired McCain's courage when they saw him on television barely able to use his legs and arms.

In 1982, McCain left the military and settled in Phoenix, Arizona. He won election to the House, and four years later he was elected to the Senate. McCain was named to "*Time*'s 25 Most Influential Americans" list in 1997. In 2006, *Time* ranked McCain as one of "America's 10 Best Senators" and one of the "*Time* 100: The People Who Shape Our World."

➔THE GINGRICH REVOLUTION

For the first time in forty years, the Republicans became the majority in the House in 1995. Newton "Newt" Leroy Gingrich from Georgia is given the most credit for leading them to victory. The House Republicans rewarded him by electing him Speaker.

Gingrich and his colleague Republican Dick Armey from Texas, proposed to Congress a plan called the *Contract With America*. The contract had two major goals. One goal was to reduce government regulation of business. The other was to shift responsibility for helping citizens to the state governments. Within one hundred days, nine of the ten items in the contract had passed in the House.

Newt Gingrich was Speaker of the House from 1995 until 1999. His Contract With America helped Republicans gain a strong majority in the House of Representatives during that time.

▲ *Robert C. Byrd from West Virginia is the longest-serving senator in the history of the U.S. Congress. He is shown here on the left, taking his ninth oath of office. Senator Jay Rockefeller is in the center, and Vice President Dick Cheney is to the right.*

Many of Gingrich's proposals failed to pass in the Senate. However, his intense effort to change the federal government is usually called the Gingrich Revolution. Gingrich ran into trouble on two fronts. He refused to negotiate with Democrats. This damaged his image with the public. Even more serious was the charge that he used money from a book contract to help finance his political campaign. Republicans decided to elect a new Speaker in 1998. As a result, Gingrich resigned from Congress.

⊛ LONGEST SERVICE IN CONGRESS

Most early members of Congress served only one or two terms. That changed in the the twentieth

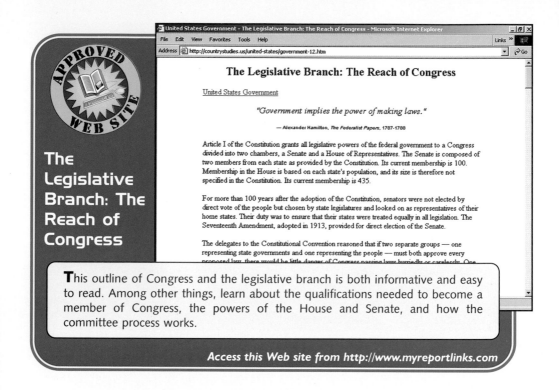

The Legislative Branch: The Reach of Congress

The Legislative Branch: The Reach of Congress

United States Government

"Government implies the power of making laws."

— Alexander Hamilton, *The Federalist Papers*, 1787-1788

Article I of the Constitution grants all legislative powers of the federal government to a Congress divided into two chambers, a Senate and a House of Representatives. The Senate is composed of two members from each state as provided by the Constitution. Its current membership is 100. Membership in the House is based on each state's population, and its size is therefore not specified in the Constitution. Its current membership is 435.

For more than 100 years after the adoption of the Constitution, senators were not elected by direct vote of the people but chosen by state legislatures and looked on as representatives of their home states. Their duty was to ensure that their states were treated equally in all legislation. The Seventeenth Amendment, adopted in 1913, provided for direct election of the Senate.

The delegates to the Constitutional Convention reasoned that if two separate groups — one representing state governments and one representing the people — must both approve every proposed law, there would be little danger of Congress passing laws hurriedly or carelessly. One

This outline of Congress and the legislative branch is both informative and easy to read. Among other things, learn about the qualifications needed to become a member of Congress, the powers of the House and Senate, and how the committee process works.

Access this Web site from http://www.myreportlinks.com

century. Today most members continue in office for several terms.

On June 10, 2006, West Virginia Democrat Robert C. Byrd became the longest serving senator in history. He began in the House. Then he was elected senator in 1958. He was also leader of his party for more than a decade. Byrd is a respected historian. He wrote an award-wining four-volume history of the Senate.

The second longest service in the Senate is held by the late Strom Thurmond, a Republican from South Carolina. When he retired on January 3, 2003, Thurmond had served more than forty-seven years. A month earlier, he had turned one hundred years old, becoming the oldest person to serve in the Senate.

Not far behind him is Democratic Senator Edward M. Kennedy from Massachusetts. He was elected to fill the seat of his brother Jack Kennedy in 1962. In April 2006, *Time* magazine named Kennedy one of "America's 10 Best Senators." Over the decades, Kennedy's "record of legislation [has affected] . . . the lives of virtually every man, woman and child in the country."[7]

In the House, the longest service goes to Democrat Jamie Whitten from Mississippi. He served for fifty-four years—from November 1941 to January 1995. Whitten died seven months after leaving office. Michigan Democrat John D. Dingell is close behind Whitten. December 13, 2005, marked his fiftieth year in the House.

Only one other congressperson has served for a half century. He is Carl Vinson, a Democrat from Georgia, who died in 1981. He held office from 1914 to 1965. In 1964, President Lyndon B. Johnson presented Vinson with the Presidential Medal of Freedom with Special Distinction for his long service to his country.

⊜ ETHNIC MINORITIES

Many minorities have been elected to Congress in the past fifty years. In the 109th Congress (serving 2005–06), there were forty-three African Americans,

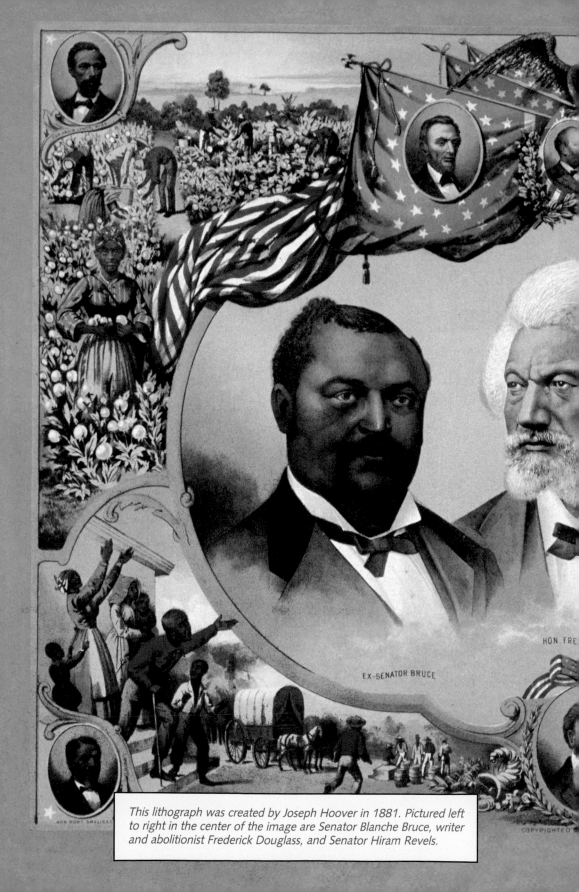

This lithograph was created by Joseph Hoover in 1881. Pictured left to right in the center of the image are Senator Blanche Bruce, writer and abolitionist Frederick Douglass, and Senator Hiram Revels.

DOUGLASS

EX-SENATOR REVELS.

STUDYING THE LESSON

HON. CHAS. E. NASH. LT.

thirty-seven Jewish Americans, twenty-eight Latino Americans, eight Asian Pacific Americans, five Arab Americans, and one American Indian.

More than one hundred African Americans have served in Congress. Twenty-two served in the Reconstruction Period after the Civil War. The first African American elected to Congress was Hiram Revels, a Republican senator from Mississippi. He served one year, from 1870 to 1871. Senator Blanche K. Bruce, a Republican from Mississippi, was the first African American to serve a full term in the Senate (March 1875 to March 1881).

The first African American elected to the Senate by popular vote was Republican Edward Brooke from Massachusetts. He served two terms—from 1967 to 1979. Only two other African Americans have been elected to the Senate. Carol Moseley-Braun, a Democrat from Illinois, was the first African-American woman elected to the Senate. She served one term, from 1993 to 1999. In the 109th Congress, there was one African-American senator, Barack Obama, a Democrat from Illinois who had been elected in 2004.

➔ BARACK OBAMA

The nation learned about Barack Obama at the Democratic National Convention in July 2004. His own history was the fulfillment of the American

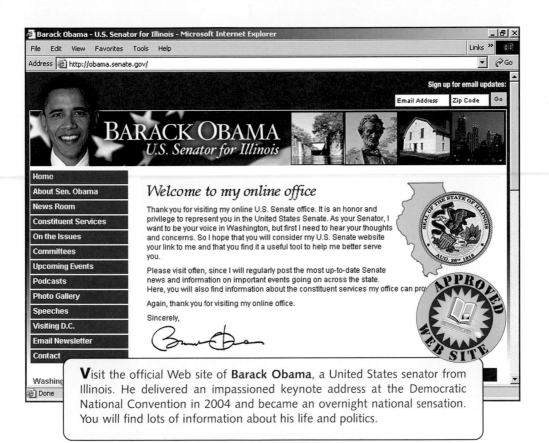

Visit the official Web site of **Barack Obama**, a United States senator from Illinois. He delivered an impassioned keynote address at the Democratic National Convention in 2004 and became an overnight national sensation. You will find lots of information about his life and politics.

Dream. His father (also named Barack Obama) was from a small village in Kenya. As a child he herded goats. His school was a shack with a tin roof. Through hard work and studying, Obama's father received a scholarship to study in America. Obama's mother was a white woman from Kansas. She met her husband while in college in Hawaii.

Obama told the cheering crowd at the convention:

> I stand here today, grateful for the diversity of my heritage, aware that my parents' dreams live on in

my precious daughters. I stand here knowing that
my story is part of the larger American story, that
I owe a debt to all of those who came before me,
and that, in no other country on earth, is my story
even possible.[8]

Obama graduated from Harvard Law School in
1992. He turned down offers to join well-known
law firms. Instead, he did community work in
Chicago. He was active in local and national
Democratic campaigns. Obama also taught constitutional law at the University of Chicago, and
served in the Illinois State Senate.

Obama appeals to voters because he gains the
trust of those who disagree with him. People
believe Obama is sincere, dependable, and honest.
In April 2006, *Time* magazine named him one of
"The Up-And-Comers" in Congress. On February
10, 2007, Obama announced his bid to become
the future Democratic candidate for president.

WOMEN IN CONGRESS

Two hundred and thirty-six women have served in
Congress: 203 in the House and 33 in the Senate.
In the 109th Congress, there were forty-six Demo-
cratic and twenty-four Republican women in the
House. The Senate had nine Democratic and five
Republican women.

California had two women in the Senate at the
same time. They are Democrats Dianne Feinstein

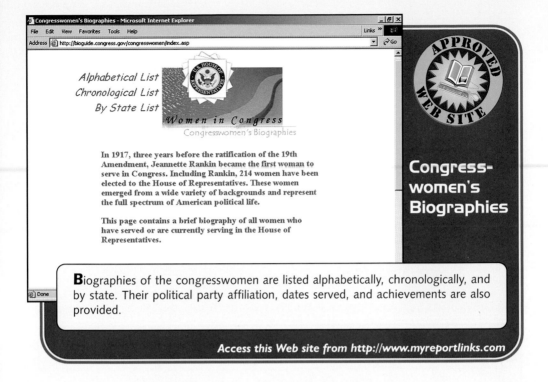

Congressmen's Biographies - Microsoft Internet Explorer

File   Edit   View   Favorites   Tools   Help   Links »

Address http://bioguide.congress.gov/congresswomen/index.asp   Go

Alphabetical List
Chronological List
By State List

Women in Congress
Congresswomen's Biographies

In 1917, three years before the ratification of the 19th Amendment, Jeannette Rankin became the first woman to serve in Congress. Including Rankin, 214 women have been elected to the House of Representatives. These women emerged from a wide variety of backgrounds and represent the full spectrum of American political life.

This page contains a brief biography of all women who have served or are currently serving in the House of Representatives.

Congress-
women's
Biographies

Done

Biographies of the congresswomen are listed alphabetically, chronologically, and by state. Their political party affiliation, dates served, and achievements are also provided.

Access this Web site from http://www.myreportlinks.com

and Barbara Boxer. Out of fifty-three House seats, California also has nineteen filled by women. This is by far the state with the most women in Congress. The Democratic leader of the House is Nancy Pelosi from California.

The first woman elected to Congress was Jeannette Rankin, a Republican from Montana. Elected to the House in 1917, she opposed America's entry into World War I. When she ran for the Senate in 1919, her antiwar views led to her defeat. She was elected to the House again in 1941. But she opposed America's entry into World War II. As a result, she was defeated in 1943.

The first woman to serve in the Senate was Democrat Rebecca Latimer Felton, from Georgia. Her husband died just before the end of Congress's term in 1922. At eighty-seven years old, she was appointed in 1922 to serve the final day of her husband's term. The first woman elected to the Senate was Hattie Wyatt Caraway, a Democrat from Arkansas. She also filled the vacancy in December 1931 left by her husband's death. She was reelected to two full terms and served until January 1945.

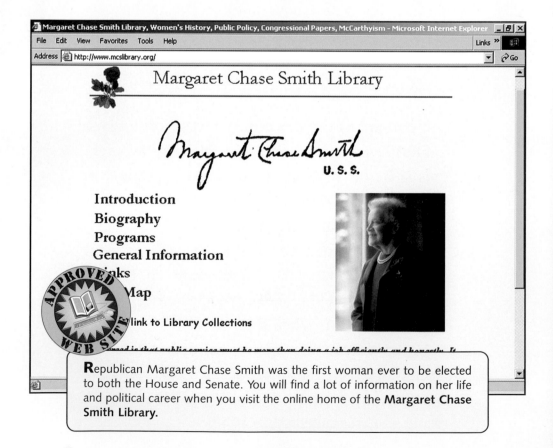

Margaret Chase Smith Library, Women's History, Public Policy, Congressional Papers, McCarthyism – Microsoft Internet Explorer

File   Edit   View   Favorites   Tools   Help   Links »

Address http://www.mcslibrary.org/   Go

Margaret Chase Smith Library

Margaret Chase Smith
U. S. S.

Introduction
Biography
Programs
General Information
Links
Map
link to Library Collections

APPROVED WEB SITE

Republican Margaret Chase Smith was the first woman ever to be elected to both the House and Senate. You will find a lot of information on her life and political career when you visit the online home of the **Margaret Chase Smith Library.**

⮕MARGARET CHASE SMITH

Republican Margaret Chase Smith from Maine was elected to fill her husband's House seat after his death in 1940. Eight years later, she became the first woman to be elected to both the House and Senate. Smith won election to the Senate for four terms before being defeated in 1972.

On June 1, 1950, Smith made her now famous "Declaration of Conscience" speech. She condemned Senator Joseph McCarthy for his groundless crusade against people he falsely accused of being Communists. Later in life she said that speech would be her legacy.[9] In 1964, Smith made history by becoming the first woman placed in nomination for the presidency by either major party. In July 1989, Smith was awarded the Presidential Medal of Freedom.

⮕HILLARY RODHAM CLINTON

Time magazine named Democrat Hillary Rodham Clinton from New York one of the "*Time* 100: The People Who Shape Our World" in 2006. She has been active in politics since her high school years. She first supported Republican candidates. However, at Wellesley College she changed over to the Democratic party. Clinton gave the address at her college graduation in 1969. *Life* magazine published a feature article on her.

Senator Hillary Rodham Clinton from New York is a former First Lady. In 2007, she announced she would seek the Democratic party's nomination to run for president in 2008.

Clinton graduated from Yale Law School in 1973. Soon after, she joined the legal staff of the House Judiciary Committee. At the time, the committee was investigating the Watergate crimes to determine if impeachment charges should be brought against President Nixon.

She married future president Bill Clinton in 1975. But she continued to practice law. Hillary Clinton was especially active in children's rights causes. *The National Law Journal* named her one of the one hundred most influential lawyers in America in 1988 and 1991.

Members of both major political parties regard Clinton as a skillful and intelligent senator. Republican Lindsey Graham says that she "is sought out by her colleagues to form legislative partnerships. . . . [and] has managed to build unusual political alliances on a variety of issues with Republicans."[10] These are skills that make her a leading presidential candidate.

WHAT THE LEGISLATURE DOES FOR AMERICANS

5

ongress determines how federal money is spent and where it is spent. Its members pass bills that affect the entire nation. Any business that operates in more than one state must abide by laws passed by Congress. These include laws that control the imports and exports at the nation's ports. Congress makes the laws on immigration and civil rights.

Much of the government's money is distributed to different states. This money helps build and repair highways and bridges. It can help revive business activity and fund scientific research.

⊕ FEDERAL BILLS

It is important for members of Congress to direct federal money back home to their state and district. They get into politics because they have a sense of public service. They want to help others. Former House Speaker Dennis Hastert, Republican from Illinois, explains.

President Lyndon Johnson sits with his wife, Claudia "Lady Bird" Johnson. When he was in Congress, Johnson was known as a savvy negotiator.

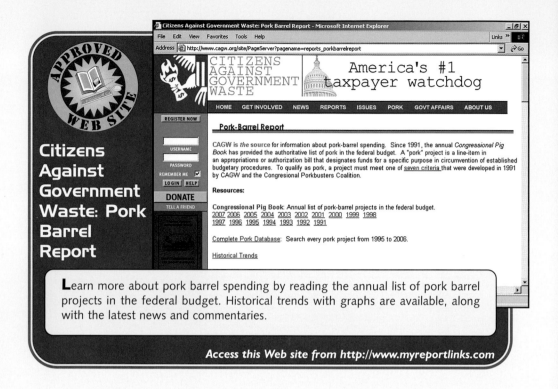

Learn more about pork barrel spending by reading the annual list of pork barrel projects in the federal budget. Historical trends with graphs are available, along with the latest news and commentaries.

Access this Web site from http://www.myreportlinks.com

"That's what members do. . . . They represent their districts. They take cases to Congress and say that 'we need this' or 'I need help here' or 'I believe that this issue should move forward.'"[1]

Congress passes two types of bills that send money back to the states and districts. One is the national bill that affects more than a single state. One of the most effective congressmen in history to get money for his district was Lyndon B. Johnson. He was described as "the best Congressman for a district that *ever was*."[2]

Johnson fashioned his skills during the Depression years. He was elected to represent the people of the Hill Country in central Texas. He was a strong supporter of President Roosevelt's New Deal program. And he was able to bring millions of dollars into his district to help the poor. In one year, 1938, he got federal grants to pave 135 miles of farm-to-market roads in one county. Johnson's credits include federal money to build dozens of new libraries and schools. An advisor for Franklin Roosevelt said that Johnson "got more projects, and more money for his district, than anybody else [in Congress]."[3]

In the late 1930s, Johnson sought a federal loan to bring electricity to the Texas Hill Country. He had been turned down by several officials. But he was able to meet with Roosevelt. Within minutes the loan was approved. Johnson was able to get almost $2 million for the local electric company to expand into the Hill Country. Soon, 1,830 miles of electric lines were being put up to provide service to nearly three thousand new customers.

EARMARKS

Each year, the federal budget details how the tax money from American citizens is to be spent. Included in each budget are smaller bills called earmarks and pork barrels. These are unlike the bills that fund national projects across the country. Earmarks and pork barrels supply funds only for local and state projects. Some of these bills are earmarked for specific purposes. They give details about who gets the money and how it will be spent.

Pork barreling is one way legislators finance pet projects for their constituents. Learn more about this type of government spending and how lobbyists are involved when you read this article.

Access this Web site from http://www.myreportlinks.com

The number of earmarks has increased rapidly, from over fourteen hundred in 1995 to almost thirteen thousand in 2005.

Most members of Congress defend earmarks. A bill might be earmarked to fund a new local community center or museum. In 2000, Republican Congressman Chip Pickering from Mississippi secured a $3 million grant for the Meridian Opera House. In 2005, Democratic Congressman Joe Baca from California got $317,000 to expand the Jack Bulik Teen Community Center in the city of Fontana. In 2006, Republican Congressman Michael Oxley got $424,000 to build new airport hangars at the Bellefontaine Regional Airport.

Congresswoman Bernice Johnson goes home to her Dallas district often to speak and present grant money for local projects. In 2006, she obtained $225,000 for the East Dallas Community Organization from the Department of Justice to fund a Weed and Seed program that would improve safety. To support that grant, she got $175,000 for the Greater Dallas Crime Commission that will help set up after-school programs for youth, job training, neighborhood cleanups, increased home ownership, and new business development.

Often representatives from the same state work closely to pass bills that help people around their state. In 2005–06, Congressman Jeff Fortenberry and other Nebraska representatives got $26 million for work on Highway 35. They also got federal funds to revive a neighborhood in the state capital, for a new building at Peru State College, and to modernize a county courthouse.

➡ PORK BARREL

Bills that are not meant to improve the lives of the public are called pork barrels. These are a waste of American tax money. Usually pork barrel bills are intended to reward people back home for their support. This helps representatives get votes in upcoming elections. Sometimes it is not easy to tell the difference between earmarks and pork.

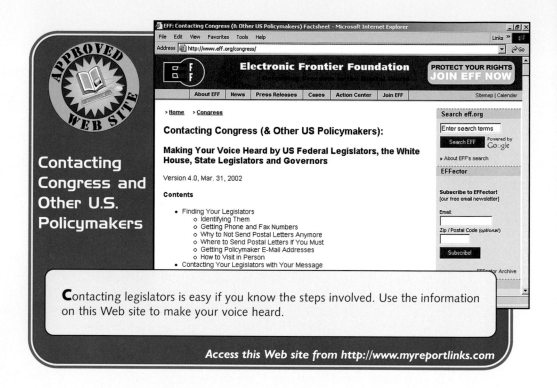

EFF: Contacting Congress (& Other US Policymakers) Factsheet - Microsoft Internet Explorer

File   Edit   View   Favorites   Tools   Help   Links »

Address   http://www.eff.org/congress/   Go

Electronic Frontier Foundation   PROTECT YOUR RIGHTS
                                             JOIN EFF NOW

About EFF | News | Press Releases | Cases | Action Center | Join EFF   Sitemap | Calendar

› Home   › Congress   Search eff.org

Contacting Congress (& Other US Policymakers):   Enter search terms

Making Your Voice Heard by US Federal Legislators, the White   Search EFF   Powered by
House, State Legislators and Governors   Google
                                                                    » About EFF's search
Version 4.0, Mar. 31, 2002
                                                                    EFFector
Contents
                                                                    Subscribe to EFFector!
  • Finding Your Legislators   [our free email newsletter]
      o Identifying Them   Email:
      o Getting Phone and Fax Numbers
      o Why to Not Send Postal Letters Anymore   Zip / Postal Code (optional)
      o Where to Send Postal Letters If You Must
      o Getting Policymaker E-Mail Addresses
      o How to Visit in Person   Subscribe!
  • Contacting Your Legislators with Your Message
                                                                    EFFector Archive

Contacting
Congress and
Other U.S.
Policymakers

Contacting legislators is easy if you know the steps involved. Use the information on this Web site to make your voice heard.

Access this Web site from http://www.myreportlinks.com

Many times pork bills give little detail about who gets the money. Other pork bills clearly are a misuse of tax money.

Few members of Congress defend pork barrels. But many still attach pork bills to larger, more important national laws passed in Congress. One example of pork is a 2002 bill that gave fifty thousand dollars to San Luis Obispo County, California, for a tattoo removal program. Another example of pork is a $150,000 grant for Therapeutic Horseback Riding in Apple Valley, California. Critics say there is no reason the American taxpayer should pay for these kinds of projects. Pork barrels can be illegal if a member of Congress gets tax payers' money to fund projects that benefit the member, family, or friends.

⇒ LOCAL OFFICES

Members of Congress spend much of their year flying back and forth between Washington, D.C., and their home states. When Congress is not in session, members go home to discuss issues with the people. They view their most important job as helping their constituency.

Members of the Senate and House get thousands of requests a year from individuals back home. To handle all the questions from the public, members of Congress have branch offices in their home state. These offices are staffed by several full-time aides. Much of their work is helping people fill out forms. Sometimes a person is not receiving Social Security checks. Or a person may need help filling out an application for veteran's benefits. More and more local offices are asked to help with immigration problems.

Republican Kay Bailey Hutchison from Texas is the fifth-highest ranking senator in her party. She has little time to deal with these individual issues. So she has offices in Austin, Dallas, Houston, San Antonio, Abilene, and Harlingen to help people. Democrat Eddie Bernice Johnson represents the Thirtieth Congressional District of Texas. This area includes parts of Dallas and small towns just south

The Library of Congress building, located in Washington, D.C. Maintaining the Library of Congress is one of the many functions the legislative branch performs.

of the city. She has two Dallas offices to handle constituents' requests.

→ CONGRESSIONAL STAFF

Congressional aides in these local offices do much of the daily work. In 1930, the total number of staff workers for all House members combined was 870. In 1967 the number was 4,055. By the 1980s and early 1990s, the number remained around 7,400. In the Senate there were 280 staff members in 1930. That number increased to 1,749 in 1967. In the 1980s and early 1990s, the number of staff for senators remained around 4,100.[4]

Congresswoman Bernice Johnson has eight full-time staff members in her two Dallas offices. In her Washington, D.C., office she has ten full-time aides.

Congressional aides must have many skills. They take on cases across a broad range of federal departments. An example of their duties can be found in a job listing from Congressman Luis V. Gutierrez of Illinois. His district includes neighborhoods in and around Chicago. The job calls for a person who can work well under pressure. The applicant must be able to speak and write well, in both English and a second language. The job requires a person who can "handle multiple tasks within a fast-paced environment" and who has the "[a]bility to work as part of a team." "Strong computer skills" are also essential.[5]

→ SERVICES TO CONSTITUENCY

Much of the help given to constituents concerns federal guidelines. Sometimes the local office can simply explain the rules. But often a problem requires the work of caseworkers. They examine and help resolve issues between the people and their government.

Local congressional offices provide help in three areas. One is local and state businesses. A second area is education. And the third area is helping people deal with government agencies.

Aides assist state and local businesses. They research and answer questions about federal guidelines. These may include rules about where smoking is allowed. Aides can help explain federal rules for hiring and worker benefits. They can also advise people how to acquire small business loans from the government. Many of these loans are offered for minorities and women who want to start their own business.

Aides also give advice on federal rules that affect education. All public schools at all levels must follow rules set by Congress. Some of these rules concern discrimination. Some deal with hiring guidelines. Other rules explain how to provide services for the physically disabled.

Many times aides are asked for help in getting federal funds to go to college. A trained aide can cut through the confusing language to help a student.

→ CASEWORK

Staff members often handle problems between constituents and federal agencies. Aides take cases in fields that they know best, such as immigration or veterans' affairs. At times, a caseworker can solve a problem with one phone call to the correct agency. Complex cases might require help from many staff members.

The first step in helping a constituent is to identify the problem. The person might have given too little information. Sometimes a person seeking help has moved but failed to notify the agency of a new address. In some cases, a person's file might be misplaced or even lost.

A caseworker has different options to choose from to solve problems. From their prior contact, most caseworkers know people at different agencies. But these contacts deal with thousands of cases a year. So caseworkers rarely meet with contacts right away. They first send an official letter to the government agency involved.

After a couple of weeks, the caseworker might phone a contact at the agency. With a phone call, the caseworker can learn when a case will be

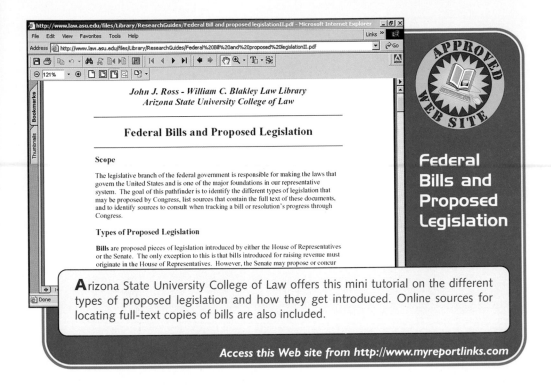

http://www.law.asu.edu/files/Library/ResearchGuides/Federal Bill and proposed legislationII.pdf - Microsoft Internet Explorer

File   Edit   View   Favorites   Tools   Help   Links »

Address   http://www.law.asu.edu/files/Library/ResearchGuides/Federal%20Bill%20and%20proposed%20legislationII.pdf   Go

John J. Ross - William C. Blakley Law Library
Arizona State University College of Law

Federal Bills and Proposed Legislation

Scope

The legislative branch of the federal government is responsible for making the laws that
govern the United States and is one of the major foundations in our representative
system. The goal of this pathfinder is to identify the different types of legislation that
may be proposed by Congress, list sources that contain the full text of these documents,
and to identify sources to consult when tracking a bill or resolution's progress through
Congress.

Types of Proposed Legislation

Bills are proposed pieces of legislation introduced by either the House of Representatives
or the Senate. The only exception to this is that bills introduced for raising revenue must
originate in the House of Representatives. However, the Senate may propose or concur

**Federal
Bills and
Proposed
Legislation**

Arizona State University College of Law offers this mini tutorial on the different
types of proposed legislation and how they get introduced. Online sources for
locating full-text copies of bills are also included.

Access this Web site from http://www.myreportlinks.com

considered. A meeting with the agency contact is
the most effective way to attempt to resolve a
case. If a meeting fails to solve the problem, caseworkers can go to their representative or senator
for help.

CASEWORK: SOCIAL SECURITY

Most casework deals with just a few federal agencies.
These include the Social Security Administration
(SSA) and the Bureau of Citizenship and Immigration Services. Other agencies citizens frequently
deal with are the U.S. Department of Health and
Human Services, the Internal Revenue Service,
and the U.S. Department of Veterans Affairs.

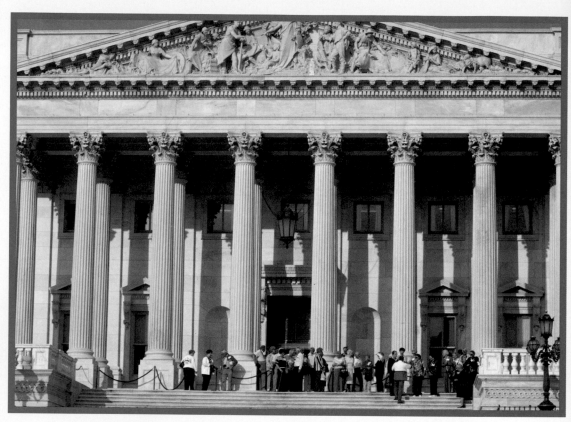

The House of Representatives building (shown here) is really one wing of the enormous Capitol building.

Almost 90 percent of American workers put a portion of their pay each month into a retirement fund called Social Security. After retirement, a person will receive monthly checks from this fund. Today, almost 15 percent of all Americans are getting checks from the SSA.

Aides deal with Social Security problems almost every day. Sometimes people do not receive their government checks. A common request is for help getting benefits that should be paid to the family of a person who has died.

The SSA gives money to workers who become disabled on the job. But there is a lot of paperwork to be filled out. The SSA has strict conditions that a person must meet to receive disability checks. Filling out the forms and waiting for the first check can take a long time. But a disabled person may need income right away. So it is common for people to seek help from their elected officials.

Republican Congresswoman Nancy Johnson has represented northwestern Connecticut since 1983. She explains a case of overdue Social Security disability payments. A man asked her office to help him prove he qualified for the money. Her staff contacted the SSA office about the claim. The SSA checked his claim at once and sent him all of his money.[6]

⊜ CASEWORK: IMMIGRATION

Immigration issues are quickly becoming a major part of the work at district and state offices. Caseworkers help noncitizens with forms to allow them to work. In other cases, they help people bring in family members from overseas. Another common request is to check the status of an immigrant's application for permanent residency or citizenship.

It takes many years for an immigrant to become a citizen. A person must live continuously in the United States for several years. This gives

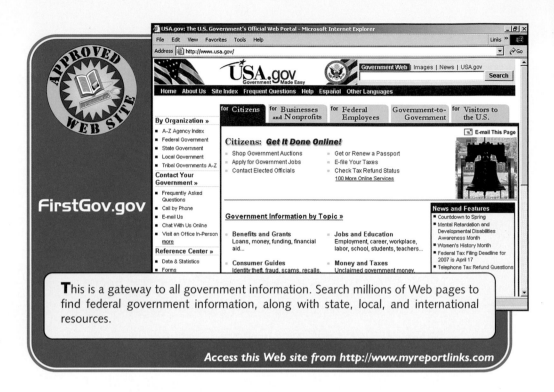

This is a gateway to all government information. Search millions of Web pages to find federal government information, along with state, local, and international resources.

Access this Web site from http://www.myreportlinks.com

the person status as a permanent resident. The ability to use English is also required. Furthermore, a person must learn the basic ideas of American history and democracy.

A person might gain citizenship for special reasons as well. Republican Congressman Christopher Shays has represented southeast Connecticut since 1987. In a recent case, a constituent was dying from leukemia in a local hospital. But he told his doctor that he wanted to become a citizen before dying.

The hospital told Shays's staff of the man's request. Shays's "office contacted the INS and found a judge to swear the man in on his death bed. The judge drove to the hospital to swear him in with his family, physicians, and hospital staff present. He became a United States citizen before he died."[7]

➔CASEWORK: LOCAL SOLUTIONS

Constituents also ask for help with problems not related to the government. These may involve mothers who need help getting children to day care. Maybe a family needs to find cheaper housing. Often aides are able to send constituents to local charities for help.

Members of Congress prefer to bypass federal agencies whenever possible. Getting local groups to help solve people's problems is often faster. Some members of Congress have set up community affairs directors to seek out local groups that can help constituents. Republican Senator Rick Santorum of Pennsylvania has a community affairs director in each of his eight regional offices. Their job is to find "faith-based and other private nonprofit groups" that can help constituents. The directors encourage people "to seek private funding, which usually is available more quickly and with less regulation."[8]

The list of local groups that can help district staff is long. These include Big Brothers and Big Sisters, Boys and Girls Clubs of America, 4-H Clubs, and churches. These and other volunteer groups often can provide immediate help to people.

Report Links

The Internet sites described below can be accessed at http://www.myreportlinks.com

▶**Documents from the Continental Congress and the Constitutional Convention**
Editor's Choice Learn more about the Continental Congress when you visit this Web site.

▶**Legislative Branch Resources on GPO Access**
Editor's Choice Find out how the federal government works.

▶**U.S. House of Representatives**
Editor's Choice This is the virtual home of the United States House of Representatives.

▶**United States Senate**
Editor's Choice The official Web site of the United States Senate.

▶**Congress for Kids: The Legislative Branch**
Editor's Choice Facts about the Legislative Branch are on this Web site.

▶**The Architect of the Capitol**
Editor's Choice Study up on the history of the Capitol building.

▶**The African American: A Journey From Slavery to Freedom**
This site is devoted to understanding the heritage of slavery.

▶**Ashland: The Henry Clay Estate**
Learn more about Senator Henry Clay on this historic landmark Web site.

▶**Barack Obama**
This is the official Web site of Senator Obama.

▶**Bill of Rights**
You can read a transcript of the Bill of Rights at this Web site.

▶**"Bush Faces Pressure to Block Port Deal"**
A CNN story on the controversy over a United Arab Emirates-based company managing United States ports.

▶**Citizens Against Government Waste: Pork Barrel Report**
Citizens Against Government Waste has posted its report on pork barrel spending.

▶**Common Cause**
These lobbyists focus on constitutional rights and citizen participation.

▶**Congresswomen's Biographies**
This guide has a biography for every congresswoman throughout history.

▶**Contacting Congress and Other U.S. Policymakers**
Find out how you can contact state and federal government officials.

Report Links

The Internet sites described below can be accessed at
http://www.myreportlinks.com

▶**Federal Bills and Proposed Legislation**
Discover more about bills and resolutions on this Web site.

▶**FirstGov.gov**
The United States government's official Web portal.

▶**The Great American Pork Barrel**
This is a *Harper's Magazine* article on pork barrel spending.

▶**House Members Who Became President or Presidential Candidates**
The Office of the Clerk has compiled this special exhibit on the history of House members.

▶**How Our Laws are Made**
This handbook provides a good description of the legislative process and rules of the House.

▶**The Legislative Branch: The Reach of Congress**
A summary of how the legislative process works is available on this Web site.

▶**The Life and Career of John Caldwell Calhoun**
View information on Calhoun and the history of African Americans at Fort Hill.

▶**The Lyndon Baines Johnson Library and Museum**
Visit one of the nation's most important presidential libraries.

▶**Margaret Chase Smith Library**
This congressional library celebrates the life of a trailblazing woman.

▶**National Security Agency**
A comprehensive and informative government site focusing on cryptology and intelligence.

▶**New Deal Network**
The Franklin and Eleanor Roosevelt Institute site is a good New Deal resource.

▶**Samuel Taliaferro Rayburn**
Browse the Texas State Historical Association's essay on Sam Rayburn.

▶**The Thirteenth Amendment: The Abolition of Slavery**
Study the Constitutional history of slavery in the United States of America.

▶**USA PATRIOT Act**
The entire text of the Patriot Act. A good primary source on the bill.

▶**U.S. Capitol**
The National Park Service offers this overview of the Capitol building.

al-Qaeda—A terrorist group started by Osama bin Laden in 1988. Its goal is to get rid of American and European influence in the Islamic world. Al-Qaeda claims credit for the September 11, 2001, attacks in New York City and Arlington, Va.

Bill of Rights—These are the first ten amendments to the Constitution of the United States. They guarantee Americans basic freedoms such as freedom of religious belief, speech, press, and assembly. They also acknowledge the right of the people to "keep and bear Arms." Other amendments protect Americans from unreasonable search and seizure of property by the government. The Bill of Rights includes protections for people accused of crimes.

checks and balances—This is a political system that divides the power of government between the different branches. In the United States, the branches are the executive, legislative, and judicial. The purpose of this system is to prevent any one branch from controlling the government.

congressional conference committee—When the Senate and House of Representatives pass two different versions of a bill, a small group of senators and representatives are appointed to a committee to work out a compromise. If they agree on the wording of the revised bill, it goes before both houses for a vote.

conservatives—A common meaning in politics is that conservatives believe most of the work being done by the federal government should be done at the state level.

Founding Fathers—This term is used to designate the men who met in 1787 in Philadelphia, wrote, debated, and approved the United States Constitution.

Great Depression—This period of American history began in 1929 and lasted through the decade of the 1930s. The American economy suffered from high unemployment, failing businesses, and a large drop in farm production.

impeachment—In American government, this term describes the process that Congress follows when it suspects public officials of misbehavior in their duties as officials.

liberals—A common meaning in politics is that liberals believe that the federal government has a duty to monitor the economy and offer economic help to people in need.

lobbyist—Someone who usually works in the nation's capital so he or she can convince members of Congress to support bills that help the members of the organization represented by the lobbyist.

The Progressive Era— This period of American history began in the 1890s and lasted to about 1920. It was a time of reform. The federal government accepted more responsibility for the welfare of the nation. Some of the laws passed led to safer food and drugs, more national parks, and women's right to vote in national elections.

Reconstruction—This period of American history began in 1865 and lasted until 1877. It was an attempt by the federal government to rebuild the South after the Civil War.

tariff—This is a tax on certain imported or exported goods. The main goal of tariffs is to encourage Americans to buy American-made products instead of products made overseas.

Chapter 1. War on Terror

1. Jonathan Karl, "Congress Vows Unity, Reprisals for Attacks," *CNN.com,* September 12, 2001, <http://archives.cnn.com/2001/US/09/11/congress.terrorism/index.html> (December 22, 2006).

2. Matt Bai, "Kerry's Undeclared War," *The New York Times Magazine,* October 10, 2004, <http://www.nytimes.com/2004/10/10/magazine/10KERRY.html?ex=1255147200&en=8dcbffeaca117a9a&ei=5090&partner=rssuserland> (December 22, 2006).

3. George W. Bush, "President's Radio Address: Homeland Security and the Patriot Act," *The White House,* December 17, 2005, <http://www.whitehouse.gov/news/releases/2005/12/20051217.html> (December 22, 2006).

4. James Risen and Eric Lichtblau, "Bush Lets U.S. Spy on Callers Without Courts," *The New York Times,* December 16, 2005, <http://www.nytimes.com/2005/12/16/politics/16program.html?ei=5090&en=e32072d786623ac1&ex=1292389200> (December 22, 2006).

5. George W. Bush, "President's Radio Address: Homeland Security and Patriot Act," The White House, December 17, 2005.

6. "Amendments to the Constitution," *The Library of Congress,* n.d., <http://memory.loc.gov/cgi-bin/ampage?collId=llsl&fileName=001/llsl001.db&recNum=144> (December 22, 2006).

7. Linda Feldmann, "Tug of War Over Presidential Powers," *The Christian Science Monitor,* December 22, 2005, <http://www.csmonitor.com/2005/1222/p01s03-uspo.html> (December 22, 2006).

Chapter 2. Congress: Organization and Responsibilities

1. James Madison, "Federalist No. 47," *The Federalist: A Commentary on the Constitution of the United States,* ed. John C. Hamilton (Washington, D.C.: Regency Pub. Inc., 1998), pp. 373–374.

2. Walter J. Olezek, *Congressional Procedures and the Policy Process,* 3rd ed. (Washington, D.C.: Congressional Quarterly Press, 1989), p. 201.

3. Barack Obama, *The Audacity of Hope* (New York: Crown, 2006), pp. 3–4.

4. "United States Constitution, Article 1, Section 8," The U.S. Constitution Online, n.d., <http://www.usconstitution.net/xconst_A1Sec8.html> (December 22, 2006).

5. Olezek, p. 230.

6. Ross Baker, *House and Senate* (New York: W.W. Norton, 1995), p. 144.

Chapter 3. History of the Legislative Branch

1. Richard D. Heffner, ed., *A Documentary History of the United States,* Expanded ed. (New York: Mentor, 1965), p. 18.

2. Robert A. Diamond, *Origins and Development of Congress* (Washington, D.C.: Congressional Quarterly Inc., 1976), pp. 182–183.

3. Jonathan Earle, "Government and Politics: The Slavery Issue: Western Politics and the Compromise of 1850," *American Eras: Westward Expansion: 1800–1860* (Detroit: Gale, 2000), p. 197.

4. Ibid.

5. William H. Seward, "Freedom in the New Territories (Appeal to a 'Higher Law')," *Classic Senate Speeches,* March 11, 1850, <http://www.senate.gov/artandhistory/history/common/generic/Speeches_Seward_NewTerritories.htm> (December 22, 2006).

6. Allan G. Bogue, "The U.S. Congress: The Era

of Party Patronage and Sectional Stress, 1829–1881," *Encyclopedia of the American Legislative System,* vol.1 (Farmington, Mich.: Charles Scribner's Sons, 1994), p. 126.

7. Alan Brinkley, *American History: A Survey,* 11th ed. (Boston: McGraw Hill, 2003), p. 672.

Chapter 4. Powerful Persons Who Have Served

1. John C. Calhoun, "Letter to James M. Mason of Virginia shortly before his death on March 31, reflecting on the Compromise of 1850," *American Studies at the University of Virginia,* September 9, 2004, <http://xroads.virginia.edu/~CAP/CALHOUN /2Ahed.html> (December 22, 2006).

2. Norman K. Risjord, "Congress in the Federalist-Republican Era, 1789–1828," *Encyclopedia of the American Legislative System,* vol. 1 (New York: Charles Scribner's Sons, 1994), p. 101.

3. Daniel Webster, "Daniel Webster's Second Reply to Hayne, 1830," *A Documentary History of the United States,* expanded ed., Richard D. Heffner ed. (New York: Mentor, 1965), p. 109.

4. Bernard A. Weisberger, "Speaking of Speakers," *American Heritage,* vol. 46, no. 4, July–August, pp. 22–24, *History Resource Center: U.S.,* Thomson Gale, May 11, 2006.

5. Quoted in H. G. Dulaney, *Speak, Mister Speaker* (Bonham, Tex.: Sam Rayburn Foundation, 1978), p. 138.

6. "Lyndon B. Johnson: Master of the Senate," *senate.gov,* n.d., <http://www.senate.gov/artandhistory /history/common/generic/People_Leaders_Johnson .htm> (December 22, 2006).

7. Massimo Calabresi and Perry Bacon, Jr., "America's 10 Best Senators," *Time,* April 24, 2006, <http://www.time.com/time/magazine/article/0,9 171,1184028,00.html> (December 22, 2006).

8. Barack Obama, "Keynote Address at the 2004 Democratic National Convention," *Barackobama.com,* July 27, 2004, <http://www.barackobama.com /2004/07/27/dnc_2004.php> (December 22, 2006).

9. "Expanded Biography," *Margaret Chase Smith Library,* April 2002, <http://www.mcslibrary.org/bio /biog.htm> (December 22, 2006).

10. Lindsey Graham, "Hillary Rodham Clinton: How She Is Reshaping U.S. Politics," *Time,* May 8, 2006, <http://www.time.com/time/magazine/article /0,9171,1187184,00.html> (March 15, 2007).

Chapter 5. What the Legislature Does for Americans

1. Jonathan Allen, "Earmark Reform: The first battle is to define the term," *The Hill,* January 25, 2006, <http://www.hillnews.com/thehill/export/ TheHill/News/Frontpage/012506/earmark1.html> (December 22, 2006).

2. Robert A. Caro, *The Years of Lyndon Johnson: The Path to Power* (New York: Alfred A. Knopf, 1982), p. 501.

3. Ibid.

4. Eric O'Keefe and Aaron Steelman, "The End of Representation: How Congress Stifles Electoral Competition," Cato Policy Analysis No. 279, *Cato Institute,* August 20, 1997, <http://www.cato.org/ pubs/pas/pa-279.html> (May 24, 2006).

5. "Job Listings & Opportunities," *Hispanic Lawyers Association of Illinois,* December 10, 2005, <http://www.hlai.org/job.htm> (May 25, 2006).

6. Nancy Johnson, "District Casework: Casework Examples," *Congresswoman Connecticut Fourth District,* n.d., <http://www.house.gov/nancyjohnson /casework.htm> (May 26, 2006).

7. Congressman Christopher Shays, "Constituent

Services: Casework Examples," *United States House of Representives,* n.d., <http://www.house.gov/shays /Constituent_Services/constituent.htm> (December 22, 2006).

8. Adam Meyerson, "A Small but Growing Group of Members of Congress Serve Their Constituents by Encouraging Private, Local Solutions to Community Problems," Policy Review, No. 88, March–April 1998, *The Heritage Foundation,* n.d., <http://www .policyreview.org/mar98/people.html> (December 22, 2006).

Brannen, Jr., Daniel E. *Checks and Balances: The Three Branches of the American Government.* Detroit: UXL, 2005.

Cunningham, Kevin. *The U.S. Congress: Who Represents You.* Chanhassen, Minn.: Child's World, 2005.

Feldman, Ruth Tenzer. *How Congress Works: A Look at the Legislative Branch.* Minneapolis: Lerner Publications, Inc., 2004.

Giddens-White, Bryon. *Congress and the Legislative Branch.* Chicago: Heinemann Library, 2006.

Gutner, Howard. *The Speaker of the House.* San Diego, Calif.: Blackbirch Press, 2003.

Harvey, Bonnie Carman. *Daniel Webster: Liberty and Union, Now and Forever.* Berkeley Heights, N.J.: Enslow Publishers, 2001.

Koestler-Grack, Rachel A. *The House of Representatives.* New York: Chelsea House, 2007.

Marx, Trish. *Jeannette Rankin: First Lady of Congress.* New York: Margaret K. McElderry Books, 2006.

Mayhew, David R. *America's Congress: Actions in the Public Sphere, James Madison through Newt Gingrich.* London: Yale University Press, 2000.

Ritchie, Donald A. *The Congress of the United States: A Student Companion.* Oxford: Oxford University Press, 2001.

Wagner, Heather Lehr. *Hillary Rodham Clinton.* Philadelphia: Chelsea House, 2004.